'Fantastic, hoı orous at times, hard-hitting but good for the soul. Pooky is a well-respected professional within the mental health field and this book high-lights her personal dilemmas connecting to her professional role. We can all relate to the lessons learnt, feelings shared and only become a better person after reading this book. Honest accounts of her personal and professional thoughts and expe-riences. Priceless! Helpful tools given to support self-refection.'
— *Ann Marie Christian, international safeguarding consultant and trainer*

'Such a valuable and practical guide to taking care of your most precious asset – your mental health. Filled with immediately rel-evant advice, based on a disarming and always honest reflection on life, this book will help huge numbers of people.'
— *Pete Wharmby, autistic author and advocate*

'This is a very accessible and practical book that anyone who has an interest in self-improvement and seeing what they may be able to do differently with their lives, would benefit from reading. Looking at the following key topics: learning, self-care, self-acceptance, life online, death and dying, love and friendship, living with anxiety, Pooky draws from personal expe-riences to support the reader through a reflective process, whilst also providing practical things to try for each topic area covered.

The book oozes humility, honesty and authenticity, and in doing so allows the reader to reflect on the topics in relation to themselves throughout. This provides a powerful and accessible approach that I wholeheartedly recommend.

I don't think you could read this book without being better after having done so...why not give it a try?'
— *Gare* 'visor :NCo

'This book is a gift for anybody struggling with their mental health or self-esteem. It's full of lessons in learning and growing, and most importantly in forgiving ourselves for living imperfect lives. Pooky shares so much wisdom, and the exercises at the end of each chapter help to personalize the learning we can take from Pooky's wealth of experience, both personal and professional. A truly wonderful resource for anyone hoping to overcome their imposter syndrome and be kinder to themselves.'
– *Cara Lisette, mental health campaigner and writer, registered mental health nurse and child cognitive behavioural therapist*

'Pooky's life lessons are a refreshing blend of shared vulnerability and hard-won wisdom. I felt myself growing as I read, and I have already started to think about the life changes I'll make in response to this apparently simple yet deeply inspiring book.'
– *Dr Kathryn Mannix, retired palliative care physician and author of* With the End in Mind *and* Listen

# Things I Got Wrong
# So You Don't Have To

*by the same author*

**The Mentally Healthy Schools Workbook**
**Practical Tips, Ideas, Action Plans and Worksheets**
**for Making Meaningful Change**
*Pooky Knightsmith*
*Foreword by Norman Lamb*
ISBN 978 1 78775 148 4
eISBN 978 1 78775 149 1

**Can I Tell You About Self-Harm?**
**A Guide for Friends, Family and Professionals**
*Pooky Knightsmith*
*Foreword by Jonathan Singer*
ISBN 978 1 78592 428 6
eISBN 978 1 78450 796 1

**The Healthy Coping Colouring Book and Journal**
**Creative Activities to Help Manage Stress, Anxiety and Other Big Feelings**
*Pooky Knightsmith*
*Illustrated by Emily Hamilton*
ISBN 978 1 78592 139 1
eISBN 978 1 78450 405 2

**Using Poetry to Promote Talking and Healing**
*Pooky Knightsmith*
*Foreword by Catherine Roche and Dr Fiona Pienaar*
ISBN 978 1 78592 053 0
eISBN 978 1 78450 323 9

**Self-Harm and Eating Disorders in Schools**
**A Guide to Whole-School Strategies and Practical Support**
*Pooky Knightsmith*
ISBN 978 1 84905 584 0
eISBN 978 1 78450 031 3

# THINGS I GOT WRONG SO YOU DON'T HAVE TO

48 Lessons to Banish Burnout
and Avoid Anxiety for Those
Who Put Others First

## Pooky Knightsmith

Foreword by Nicola Brentnall

**Jessica Kingsley Publishers**
London and Philadelphia

For Grant, who loves me just as I am.

# Contents

## Part 4: Lessons in Life Online

## Part 5: Lessons in Death and Dying

## Part 6: Lessons in Living with Anxiety

## Part 7: Lessons in Love and Friendship

# Foreword

It is an honour to write this Foreword for a dear friend and fellow traveller along the pot-holed highway of life. I have known Pooky for ten years and I have enjoyed her friendship and advice while she and I have both held demanding and challenging leadership roles as Directors, CEOs and Trustees. We have walked together through great days and dark times. I value her friendship more than I can say. I have travelled the world in pursuit of my work in youth-led international development and have been lucky to meet some truly exceptional people. Without hesitation, one of the most exceptional of all is Pooky.

*Northern Lights*, the first in Philip Pullman's masterpiece His Dark Materials, contains a moment that I think is perfect for the beginning of this, Pooky's remarkable book. I say this because, like me, you may have come to these pages looking for answers to problems, some of which may have beset you for years. At the end of *Northern Lights*, the heroine, Lyra, walks into the sky, brave and resolute, towards a whole new world. Her purpose is to right grievous wrongs brought about by others and to fix mistakes she feels she, too, has made. In doing so, she chooses to face the future, and leave the past behind. That Pooky continues to write about mental health, and her own health and struggles to help other people, makes her for me a real-life Lyra – fearless, resolute, determined to use her knowledge and experience, even at considerable personal cost, to lift people, to help them to put things right and to live again.

I first knew Pooky in her absence, rather than her presence. At the time, I had just joined the Board of an eating disorders charity. As a survivor myself, I was keen to find some way that I could bring my experience of charity leadership to an organization that needed practical help, some TLC and a reboot. At Board meetings, where Trustees drafted the future of the organization, like Macavity, Pooky wasn't there. We did not know, but it was a time when, in her own words, she was 'falling down the rabbit hole' of a mental health crisis. None of us had any real idea of what she was going through. But when she could, she sent in observations, ideas, or even just a single insight on an issue we were considering. Every nugget was useful, every idea thoughtful, generous, kind. As a newbie, I was intrigued by our absent friend, and watched the other Trustees who knew her defend her fiercely. And over the weeks and months that followed, it became crystal clear to me why they did. Not only is Pooky exceptional in so many ways, she also truly understands the assignment. She has lived the experience and has ideas, suggestions, tactics and methods to help people tackle and overcome the challenges they face. Her insights were to us then, and to so many now, simply invaluable.

Reader, you have chosen well. You will find this to be a very clever and very kind book, packed with good things. Pooky shares with us her experience, insights which are extraordinarily helpful. With raw honesty, she shares with us how she tackled issues of insecurity, suicidal ideation, anorexia and anxiety in ways that reach out with great love and understanding to those facing similar challenges. She covers the highs and lows we all experience, like love, loss, children, families and more. This book gives us techniques to deal with the challenges we face in our own lives and to accept ourselves for who we are, without reproach. Many of us won't have been through all the things that Pooky has – but we are all human, with insecurities and worries, with regrets, hopes, toxic friendships, dreams and doubts of our own. This book has something for us all.

You can dip into the book as you choose, in any sequence, for the message you may need in any moment. Here you will find freedom to move where you need when you need. You will find insight in little doses precisely measured to help you pause, breathe, reset and go again. I found the consistency in the format of each chapter to be like hand-holds on climbing walls. In reading each section, I was able to pull myself up and up, away from the uncertainty and towards the summit of each problem. Pooky is a climber too, and writes 'together we climb, we fall, we succeed, we fail, and all with a smile on our faces and getting a little stronger each time'. We are all a work in progress. And that's OK.

In His Dark Materials, Philip Pullman talks about finding courage to turn away from old ways to seek and find new worlds, where we learn, understand and grow. With this book, we can all be better equipped to do this, to grow in confidence, to shed the doubts of the past and embrace new possibilities and new worlds.

So, let's go with Pooky/Lyra. Let's read on and walk into the sky, towards the potential that awaits us all.

Nicola Brentnall MVO, MSc
CEO, Ajaz.org
@NicolaBrentnall

# Introduction

I have spent much of my adult life educating people, specifically about how to support children and young people facing mental health challenges or living with special needs. I love my work and I love that people trust me to share ideas with them that can enable them to flourish in their roles working with or caring for children.

But a peculiar thing has happened in recent years. More and more people are looking for me to share advice, ideas and guidance based not on the years of research, study and working in the field I've done, but rather on my own experience. This is especially puzzling because, honestly, I feel as if I'm muddling through at best.

But people are curious and I often find that the ideas I share in an attempt at trying to do a little better at this thing called life are often the ideas which people most readily engage with. So...this book is a radical departure from anything which I've written before. It's kind of all about me. It's all about you too because I'm hoping that by sharing some of my experiences, ideas and bumps in the road, I can help you to do some things a little bit differently too.

Unlike everything else I've written, this is not steeped in research. It's not underpinned by any evidence base other than the fact that, quite surprisingly, I'm still alive; and finally I think I'm starting to thrive.

I feel pretty self-conscious writing this; it's harder than the kind of stuff I normally write. But I hope it strikes a chord. Please be kind in your response to the words within. Remember that they're written by a person. A real human being who just wants to make life a little bit better for other people and who, despite appearances, is plagued by insecurity.

Enjoy...and if you find any of the lessons helpful, please tweet me @PookyH and maybe share some ideas of your own too.

Love
Pooky

For those of you who don't like to write on books, the 'Things you could try' sections at the end of each chapter are available to download from https://library.jkp.com/ redeem using the voucher code: NVCWGEU

Part 1

# LESSONS IN LEARNING

# Use life's lessons to create a new path, not to muddy an old one

Sometimes, new knowledge can make us regretful of what we've said or done in the past. It is far better to forge ahead equipped with new knowledge than to ruminate on what we could or should have done differently, if only we'd known.

## What I got wrong in the past

We are all learning new things every day and with new knowledge comes new responsibilities to use that new knowledge or the skills or ideas you've gained to tread a new path. This is exciting and wonderful, with each new lesson in life providing us with an opportunity for a brighter future. However, the temptation can be to judge our past selves based on our current knowledge. This is a road to true misery. No matter how hard we may wish to, we cannot change the past; but we can spend a lot of time wishing we'd done things differently.

## The lesson and the teacher

This is a lesson that I first learned from my therapist, Mat. I'm sure he's far from the only therapist to impart this wisdom but he was the person from whom I learned it and it's a lesson for which I've been very grateful and which I try to share often. During the course of therapy, and looking back as well as forward, we can often find ourselves ruminating on what we've got wrong in the past. We dwell on the 'if onlys' and hold our past selves to account based on the skills, knowledge and information we have now. Mat would remind me often, as I looked backwards and was scathing of my teenage self's inability to create a different ending, that I made the best decisions I could at the time. Like many victims of rape and abuse, I blamed myself and it took a lot of therapy before I learned to see the actions of my early teenage self as those of a child who was scared and alone.

## What I do now

This is an important lesson to start this book with because it's possible that some of the ideas in here will land well with you and you might find yourself wanting to think or behave a little differently in the future. Perhaps something will click and you'll look back at how you used to do things and wish you'd known then what you know now. But you didn't. So forgive yourself and instead look forward and plan how you'll use your new learning to create an ever-so-slightly brighter future rather than being weighed down by a past which is beyond your control to change.

This lesson is also an important one I weave into my work every day as I spend a lot of time teaching people about how they can support children and young people who are struggling with challenges. While the ideas I share are simple, they are often groundbreaking for those who start to use them. This is wonderful, and a parent, nurse or teacher who's able to support a child to stop self-harming or whose new strategies mean that an autistic child finds the day-to-day of school less traumatic is someone who should feel joyous in their new knowledge. But, often, people look back. They consider the harm their previous approaches might have caused and they feel sad, angry or frustrated with themselves. So I try every day to remind people to look forward, not back, often repeating Mat's words to me. You made the best decisions you could at the time. Onwards.

## Looking ahead

One of the things I'm trying to move towards in my own personal and professional life is to share more widely my own feelings about what I've done wrong in the past because I didn't have the information then that I have now. It can make me feel quite vulnerable as a leader of learning when I say, 'Hey this thing I used to teach you...forget that... We know more now and what I said before is wrong', but it's the right thing to do. A recent example was sharing with my network papers about why we no longer advocate proxy methods for people who self-harm (things like snapping elastic bands on the wrist). I was devastated to learn that methods I'd advocated widely in the past were not only ineffective but could be doing harm. But at the time I was advocating those ideas, they were our best guess. We've learned more since and it's vital that neither my ego nor my shame gets in the way of me sharing these new lessons with my network and their networks in turn.

## THINGS YOU COULD TRY

Here are some things you could try if you'd like to apply this lesson to your own life:

1.  **Commit to looking forward not backward** – try to catch yourself each time you learn something new and try to encourage your first thought always to be 'What can I do next with this?' rather than 'How did I get this wrong in the past?'

    *Make a start by* writing down a regret or misgiving you have about something you've done or an approach you've taken and think about what you can do differently next time:

    *What I got wrong:*

    . . . . . . . . . . . . . . . . . . . . . . . . . . . . . . . . . . . . . . . . . . . . . . . . . . . . . . . . . .

    . . . . . . . . . . . . . . . . . . . . . . . . . . . . . . . . . . . . . . . . . . . . . . . . . . . . . . . . . .

    . . . . . . . . . . . . . . . . . . . . . . . . . . . . . . . . . . . . . . . . . . . . . . . . . . . . . . . . . .

*What I could do differently next time:*

. . . . . . . . . . . . . . . . . . . . . . . . . . . . . . . . . . . . . . . . . . . . . . . . . . . . . . .

. . . . . . . . . . . . . . . . . . . . . . . . . . . . . . . . . . . . . . . . . . . . . . . . . . . . . . .

. . . . . . . . . . . . . . . . . . . . . . . . . . . . . . . . . . . . . . . . . . . . . . . . . . . . . .

2. **Acknowledge any discomfort you're holding and try to let it go** – there may be past lessons which have sat uncomfortably with you and that you find your thoughts turning to periodically. Let your thoughts go there and sit with the knowledge that you did things differently from the way you'd do them now, but you did the best you could at the time. Writing it down and forgiving yourself in writing can be surprisingly healing.

   *Make a start by* noting down three things you think it is time to forgive yourself for:

   1. . . . . . . . . . . . . . . . . . . . . . . . . . . . . . . . . . . . . . . . . . . . . . . . . . . .

   2. . . . . . . . . . . . . . . . . . . . . . . . . . . . . . . . . . . . . . . . . . . . . . . . . . . .

   3. . . . . . . . . . . . . . . . . . . . . . . . . . . . . . . . . . . . . . . . . . . . . . . . . . . .

3. **When you teach others new things, bear in mind that they may feel this way too** – when you're in the fortunate position of being able to impart lessons to others, consider that this may affect them too. Tackle this head on, talk about it, acknowledge it and give them permission to move on.

# The more you know, the less you think you know

The more we learn about something, the more we realize there is still much to learn. Instead of aiming for a complete knowledge in a topic, we should embrace an 'always learning' mindset.

## What I got wrong in the past

I used to believe people who told me they knew the answers. I used to think that if I worked hard for a long time, I would know the answers. I've come to realize – sometimes by putting my faith in the wrong places and people – that there is always more to learn and that those who profess to know the answers rarely do, while those who are open about how much more they have to learn about a topic are frequently great sources of wisdom.

## The lesson and the teacher

I learned this lesson very early in my career, back while I was still studying for my PhD at the Institute of Psychiatry at King's College London. Little did I know it at the time, but I'd landed among the rock stars of the world in which I was studying and had as my PhD supervisors two professors, Ulrike and Janet, whose names would open relevant doors anywhere in the world. As I got to know them and became aware of their standing and the huge knowledge they had between them, I began to feel a little daunted. I wondered what I could possibly bring to this amazing clinical team. Then one day, my place became clear.

The BBC wanted to interview Janet or Ulrike about my work. They didn't want to interview me as I didn't have the credentials of professor or doctor at the time; but Ulrike and Janet declined the interview saying that they didn't know enough to do a good job and that the BBC needed either me or no one at all. I was floored at the time and remember saying, 'But of course you know enough, you know so much!', and they explained to me very simply that having a great depth of knowledge in a particular field made you very aware of your limitations.

They had brought me on board specifically to work within the education sector while their expertise was within health. However little I felt like it at the time, I really was the expert here. I explained my insecurities, saying that even if the BBC had chosen to interview me, I'd have felt that I too wouldn't have known enough. Ulrike and Janet exchanged a glance at this point and told me I would become a great researcher.

## What I do now
From then on, I stopped trying to know everything about any given topic and rather embraced my role as a learner, delighting in the things I didn't know and wondering always where I could find out more. This had been my best mode of learning as a child (in fact, I recall our psychology teacher having to occasionally have 'no questions from Pooky today' lessons when we were trying to finish the syllabus or revise a topic quickly!). As an adult, I think I'd got lost somewhere along the way and felt that I should know all the answers.

## Looking ahead
I'm increasingly wary of people who claim to be the expert in a topic, especially if they have narrow-minded views and prescribe particular ways of doing things without an openness to trying other methods or adapting ideas for differing circumstances. Instead, I look to people who are less secure in their knowledge

but whose actions reveal someone who has learned a lot and who is still learning.

Where I have the chance to create a stage for someone to share knowledge, I increasingly try to be 'expertise-led rather than expert-led' – a mantra I turn to often in my role directing Creative Education. We teach thousands of people every week, often school leaders, and when choosing someone to host a webinar on a particular topic I look first to practitioners currently grappling with the particular problem we're trying to address. There is always someone who purports to be the expert in the topic, but rarely do I ask them to lead a session. Instead, I turn to school staff who feel that they don't have much to give and still have a lot to learn, and who are worried about not doing a good enough job.

They are almost universally brilliant.

## ⬇ THINGS YOU COULD TRY

Here are some things you could try if you'd like to apply this lesson to your own life:

1. **Consider where your true 'expertise' lies** – the answers can sometimes be surprising. By exploring the knowledge, skills and passions that others look to you for advice on, you can often see which parts of you people most value. These may differ from the domains of knowledge in which you feel most secure. Often people learn most from others who are currently facing similar challenges and haven't figured out all the answers yet.

   *Make a start by* noting down the things people have recently asked for your advice or ideas on:

   1. ............................................................

   2. ............................................................

   3. ............................................................

**4.** . . . . . . . . . . . . . . . . . . . . . . . . . . . . . . . . . . . . . . . . . . . . . . . . . . . . . . . .

**5.** . . . . . . . . . . . . . . . . . . . . . . . . . . . . . . . . . . . . . . . . . . . . . . . . . . . . . . . .

*What surprised you?*

. . . . . . . . . . . . . . . . . . . . . . . . . . . . . . . . . . . . . . . . . . . . . . . . . . . . . . . .

. . . . . . . . . . . . . . . . . . . . . . . . . . . . . . . . . . . . . . . . . . . . . . . . . . . . . . . .

. . . . . . . . . . . . . . . . . . . . . . . . . . . . . . . . . . . . . . . . . . . . . . . . . . . . . . . .

2. **Question the 'expert' label** – what makes someone an expert? Often, it's simply the fact that they confidently tell us they are one. Some of these experts may be fantastic but waiting in the wings may be a whole range of other people whose ideas and experience will be of even more use to you if only you can make space to hear from them.

3. **Always be learning** – don't give up on a topic that you don't feel you have mastery of, but understand that it's only as you become more competent and knowledgeable about a topic that you begin to realize how much more there is to learn. Enjoy the learning journey while understanding that it's one that never ends.

   *Make a start by* reflecting on areas of passion, intrigue and interest to you that you'd like to commit to learning more about.

   *I'd like to learn more about:*

   . . . . . . . . . . . . . . . . . . . . . . . . . . . . . . . . . . . . . . . . . . . . . . . . . . . . . . . .

   . . . . . . . . . . . . . . . . . . . . . . . . . . . . . . . . . . . . . . . . . . . . . . . . . . . . . . . .

   . . . . . . . . . . . . . . . . . . . . . . . . . . . . . . . . . . . . . . . . . . . . . . . . . . . . . . . .

# Brilliant people struggle with imposter syndrome too

That feeling that everyone is going to figure out that you don't really know what you're talking about? Everyone gets it, even the people you'd least expect.

## What I got wrong in the past

I grew up in very different circumstances from those in which I now live. Neither of my parents even considered going to university, but I eventually ended up with a PhD. At every step along the way, I thought that today would be the day that everyone figured out I really shouldn't be here. That feeling that I wasn't good enough, wasn't deserving, has somehow plagued me throughout my life. I thought it was just me, a 'poor girl done good' thing that meant that just as I found multiple sets of cutlery confusing to navigate, had no idea what to do with a napkin and found courgettes and avocados decidedly exotic, I found life kind of confusing too. I thought it was part of my make-up and background.

Often baffled, but rarely undeterred, I went on. The harder I worked, the more I found that people listened to me, and the more I wondered why.

## The lesson and the teacher

I kept these thoughts to myself for the longest time, somehow convincing myself that if I were to admit to feeling like an imposter in my own life and uncertain in my own knowledge, this admission would cause the scales to fall away from others' eyes and they would see me for the fake I am. But during the pandemic, I had a bit of a turning point. In the course of my work, I spoke to a lot of teachers who, after a long lockdown-enforced hiatus from teaching face-to-face, were due to return to the classroom and had lost all confidence in their ability to do so. Quite a few people within my network privately confided their fears in me, asking for advice on how to manage. The thing is, everyone thought it was just them...just as for many years I'd thought it was just me.

So I started the conversation on social media. I let the world know that anyone who was feeling a sense of imposter syndrome was not alone; that everyone was secretly feeling it and if only we could be brave enough to break our silence we'd find we were among friends here. Not alone, but in glorious company. People responded in their hundreds. And it wasn't just the new teachers, there were teachers who'd taught for decades who shared of their fears of returning to the classroom every single year after the long summer break.

And together, everybody muddled through, and where there had once been silence, there was support.

## What I do now

I no longer feel alone in my feelings of imposter syndrome, and I no longer chase after the next qualification that will make me feel that I know enough. I never will, and that's okay. Instead of just squashing down those fears, I talk about them. I seek solidarity in my imposter syndrome sisters and I acknowledge that many of the people I hugely admire in life, and who I think could never possibly feel this way too, do. I know because they've told me. It seems that being a professor, having the queen as a boss, writing a dozen books or winning Olympic gold medals is not enough to make you feel absolutely sure of yourself every day.

## Looking ahead

Now that I've realized that imposter syndrome is a pretty normal feeling, I try to embrace it. I talk about it, I try to minimize the impact it has on me by asking people to help me or keeping things light and humorous. If someone is commissioning me to do a specific piece of work I now simply ask, 'Why are you asking me?' I'm sure it sometimes looks as if I'm fishing for compliments but on days when I'm genuinely baffled why someone would pay for my expertise in a certain topic, I find it helpful to understand their motives. The answers can sometimes be surprising – and it ultimately helps me to do a better job.

I no longer try to work my way through imposter syndrome. I will never be qualified enough not to feel baffled every time I have the undivided attention of a room full of people, but instead of making it all about me, I now make it all about them and it's something I advise trainers I'm coaching to do too. Sometimes we doubt ourselves and find the flaws and think we're not good enough; but if the people we're teaching took something valuable away from what we had to say, then we did a good enough job. End of.

## 🔽 THINGS YOU COULD TRY

Here are some things you could try if you'd like to apply this lesson to your own life:

1. **Start the conversation** – if you can be brave enough to talk to friends or colleagues about your feelings of imposter syndrome, you'll be amazed by how very not alone you are. You'll be in great company and you'll also have a new bunch of people right by your side cheering you on through the tricky days.

   *Make a start by* considering who you could have this conversation with. Write down the names of friends or colleagues you'd like to be brave enough to broach this with:

1. . . . . . . . . . . . . . . . . . . . . . . . . . . . . . . . . . . . . . . . . . . . . . . . . . . . . . . . . . . .

2. . . . . . . . . . . . . . . . . . . . . . . . . . . . . . . . . . . . . . . . . . . . . . . . . . . . . . . . . . . .

3. . . . . . . . . . . . . . . . . . . . . . . . . . . . . . . . . . . . . . . . . . . . . . . . . . . . . . . . . . . .

4. . . . . . . . . . . . . . . . . . . . . . . . . . . . . . . . . . . . . . . . . . . . . . . . . . . . . . . . . . . .

5. . . . . . . . . . . . . . . . . . . . . . . . . . . . . . . . . . . . . . . . . . . . . . . . . . . . . . . . . . . .

2. **Use humour to help you** – if you find yourself in a situation where you feel less than good enough and it's making you feel anxious, try to inject a little humour into the situation. I often find that this can really help to break the ice. Being a little humble and very human is a great way to build connections with a roomful of people. In my experience, it also means that you change people's expectations of you, and this somehow lightens the burden and makes it all feel more possible.

3. **Make it less about you and more about your audience** – try to reframe things so that instead of focusing on why you're not good enough to be doing this job, you focus on what your audience is getting out of it. Objective measures can really help here; on my trickier days, I find reading comments from people explaining how they're using my training sessions can remind me that my work is having more impact than I might imagine.

*Make a start by* noting down positive comments you've received recently and return to this when you receive new comments. You'll be surprised how quickly they rack up and how much better returning to these comments will make you feel on a bad day:

. . . . . . . . . . . . . . . . . . . . . . . . . . . . . . . . . . . . . . . . . . . . . . . . . . . . . . . . . . .

. . . . . . . . . . . . . . . . . . . . . . . . . . . . . . . . . . . . . . . . . . . . . . . . . . . . . . . . . . .

. . . . . . . . . . . . . . . . . . . . . . . . . . . . . . . . . . . . . . . . . . . . . . . . . . . . . . . . . . .

...............................................................

...............................................................

...............................................................

...............................................................

...............................................................

...............................................................

...............................................................

...............................................................

...............................................................

...............................................................

...............................................................

...............................................................

...............................................................

...............................................................

...............................................................

...............................................................

...............................................................

...............................................................

...............................................................

...............................................................

...............................................................

...............................................................

# If you don't know the answer, say 'I don't know the answer'

It's okay not to know the answers all the time. It's what we do next that really matters. Being willing to admit that we don't know everything and going on to problem-solve out loud can be brilliant role-modelling.

## What I got wrong in the past

It sounds so obvious that if we don't know the answer to something we should just admit that we don't know...but it's not something that comes naturally to many of us. Particularly if we're being portrayed as some kind of specialist, expert or senior, we may feel that we really should be able to answer people's questions.

The problem with this is that when people are looking to us for guidance and they respect our opinion, if we make up an answer simply to save face, our audience is likely to put more weight on that answer than it truly deserves. This holds true, I think, whether you're a professor leading a seminar or a parent talking to your child. Where there is any kind of imbalance of power, if we don't know the answer we really need to say so.

## The lesson and the teacher

Of all the role models I could point to here, I think the person who most epitomizes not knowing with grace is my friend and colleague Gareth. He works in special needs and has oodles of experience. I often feel that what Gareth doesn't know isn't worth knowing. When we were due to speak at a big event in a country I was unfamiliar with a few years ago, I remember saying to Gareth, 'What if I don't know the answers?', and his face broke into his beautiful beaming smile and he said, 'Well how about you say "I don't know"? You don't have to know all the answers all the time you know.' And I realized after this that Gareth often says 'I don't know' but he always has suggestions of where to go or who to ask.

He's been a brilliant role model to me and to many, knowing just where his expertise ends and where it's appropriate to champion others, and I aspire to be that kind of role model too. I started right away, on that trip. 'How can we support students who self-harm or have thoughts of suicide when it is illegal for us to teach or talk about these things?' I was asked by a member of school staff who looked around her, clearly fearful of having even this conversation. The honest answer, in that moment, in a country and culture that was new to me, was simply...I don't know. But that teacher and I were able to begin asking questions that aided both of our thinking. She also said she found it reassuring just being able to share her concern and have a safe space in which to explore it. Sometimes you don't need to know all the answers to make a difference to someone; sometimes you need to give them space to think.

## What I do now

When I knew less, I used to readily suggest answers to questions about which I probably didn't really know enough to share an evidenced opinion. I'm pretty good at thinking on my feet and years of the tutorial system at university means I can be pretty convincing on topics in which my knowledge is only a textbook deep. I realized over time, though, that I have a responsibility to those who trust me, who learn from me and who follow me, to be more honest about what I do and don't know.

When I don't know the answers, I try to problem-solve out loud, thinking about who or where I could turn to for trusted answers and considering what further questions might need answering. If I'm supporting an individual, I'll ask them open-ended questions and try to prompt their thinking. I often find that people who come to me for answers are often seeking reassurance, solidarity or a safe space to think out loud. In particular, adults who've got a close working or personal relationship with a child will often have great ideas about what to do next but simply haven't had a safe space (or any space) to explore or share them. In this instance, I see my role as one of ideas facilitator rather than answer bringer.

## Looking ahead

I love to learn new things and one of the best outcomes from any training session I run is being asked a question I don't know the answer to, but which I'm determined to work out. I used to be terrified of such questions, thinking that an inability to answer would lead me to be unveiled as a fake with less knowledge than I was being paid to have (thank you, imposter syndrome), but these days I embrace the tricky questions.

I'm also very lucky to have an amazing network of people around me who are always keen to share their ideas, expertise and resources. If you follow me on social media, you'll see I quite often put questions out to my network on a whole range of topics. The questions are incredibly varied; in the last few months they have ranged from 'What are good skin care products for an autistic adolescent boy?' to 'Where can I get support for a child who has Down syndrome and depression?' to 'Can you share a good workload policy with me?' It's no wonder I don't know all the answers. In sharing these questions via social media, I'm able to help the person who's asking and also myself and a whole bunch of other people along the way.

The old me would have just sent an answer to the best of my understanding. The newer me sees every question as a little explorative adventure just waiting to happen. The interesting thing is that it seems there rarely is 'an answer' but rather many different ideas and points of view, many of which are really valuable contributions.

So what does all this mean? I think it means that the thing that most used to scare me – being asked a question I couldn't answer – is now one of the things that most excites me in my day-to-day work, as every difficult question is an opportunity for connection and learning.

## ⬇ THINGS YOU COULD TRY

Here are some things you could try if you'd like to apply this lesson to your own life:

1. **Think about what kind of role model you want to be** – how would you like those you live with or work with to respond when asked a question they don't know the answer to? Do you role-model this? (Spoiler alert: the answer is often no.)

   *Make a start by* noting down what kind of role model you'd like to be:

   . . . . . . . . . . . . . . . . . . . . . . . . . . . . . . . . . . . . . . . . . . . . . . . . . . . . . . . . . . . .

   . . . . . . . . . . . . . . . . . . . . . . . . . . . . . . . . . . . . . . . . . . . . . . . . . . . . . . . . . . . .

   . . . . . . . . . . . . . . . . . . . . . . . . . . . . . . . . . . . . . . . . . . . . . . . . . . . . . . . . . . . .

   . . . . . . . . . . . . . . . . . . . . . . . . . . . . . . . . . . . . . . . . . . . . . . . . . . . . . . . . . . . .

   . . . . . . . . . . . . . . . . . . . . . . . . . . . . . . . . . . . . . . . . . . . . . . . . . . . . . . . . . . . .

2. **Commit to saying 'I don't know'** – it can be a big culture shift if you're not used to admitting your fallibility. Commit to simply being honest the next few times you find yourself in this situation and you will notice that the world does not end.

   *Make a start by* noting down each time you say 'I don't know' in the coming days or weeks:

   . . . . . . . . . . . . . . . . . . . . . . . . . . . . . . . . . . . . . . . . . . . . . . . . . . . . . . . . . . . .

..............................................................

..............................................................

..............................................................

..............................................................

3. **Hone your problem-solving skills and sources** – one of the problems with pretending we know the answers is that we don't get much chance to actually problem-solve. Stop and have a think about who and what are your trusted sources of support and, if you don't have many good ones, reach out to trusted friends or colleagues next time you find yourself in an 'I don't know' scenario and ask them to share theirs.

*Make a start by* listing your current sources of support and considering who could be added to the list:

..............................................................

..............................................................

..............................................................

..............................................................

..............................................................

# Mistakes are precious gifts that should be shared and learned from

> If instead of hiding our mistakes we celebrate them, we enable others to learn from them without having to repeat them.

## What I got wrong in the past

I'm sure that the further you read into this book, the more you wonder how I have any professional standing at all (me too!). But this lesson is about another classic mistake I've made in the past. Just as I used to feel a need to bluff my way out of situations that I didn't know the answer to, I also used to think that mistakes and failures should be hidden, brushed away, never spoken of again and swiftly moved on from.

I was wrong. I remember as a child that our junior school secretary, Mrs Childs, had a sign in her office that said 'You will never learn if you don't make mistakes'. I looked at this sign a lot as I used to spend many lunchtimes in her office on phone duty while she went to get her lunch. On reflection, I'm baffled as to why a junior school child would be trusted with this duty but I thought it was brilliant as I got to sit in her swivel chair. I didn't have to go in the playground, which I *hated*, and when the phone rang I got to take down messages, which made me feel incredibly grown up and important. I digress. I looked at this sign about the value of mistakes a lot, but despite repeated exposure to it I didn't believe it. I was quite the perfectionist as a child and was intolerant of both my own mistakes and those of others.

I worked hard not to make mistakes, and if I did make them, I hid them. But as an adult, and one who learns every day from the things I do less than perfectly, I began to realize that Mrs Childs was a lot wiser than me (even if she was daft enough to leave a nine-year-old manning the phones).

## The lesson and the teacher

When it comes to leaning into mistakes, the turning point came for me while I was studying for my PhD. I came to realize that the only research that ever sees the light of day is the research that is successful. It was an invitation from a professor called Ron that got me really thinking about this. After I sent him a query about a study he'd conducted and told him a little about my own work, he invited me to meet him at his university offices so we could discuss the answer to my question and he could share with me all the studies that hadn't worked out, the mistakes he'd made and the failures that weren't officially documented anywhere. This was the day I learned about the power of 'grey literature' – all the studies that go unpublished. Even when a study goes to plan and the results are positive, academics can have a battle on their hands to get it published, with journals often reflecting current trends and publishing biases. When a study doesn't go to plan, the chances of anyone even trying to publish or otherwise share it diminish greatly; it just doesn't make for great reading and is unlikely to be picked up and approved by editors.

Ron was coming to the end of his career and the area of mental health in schools which we were both interested in was a very small niche at the time, so I was really excited at the opportunity to learn from him. Of course, we talked about what had gone well and his many publications, but these were studies I could easily learn about by reading journals. What I could not learn from as readily were his mistakes. But here, he insisted, is where the true progress was made. And what's more, he told me, if he didn't share with me these mistakes then perhaps I'd spend precious time and resources repeating them. Academic journals do not make space for what doesn't work and so we have to find other ways of sharing and discovering it.

Ron taught me a valuable lesson and it stuck with me, coming, as it did, from someone I so admired and respected.

A few years later, I gave a presentation at an academic conference held at Reading University which explored why we should all be more willing to share our research failures. Afterwards, several researchers approached me telling me about the mistakes they'd made and the lessons they'd learned from the research studies that didn't go to plan, but how their publication history would not be a litany of these woes but rather an airbrushed summary of what went well. There's still a long way to go but we can each play a small part in trying to change this culture.

## What I do now

I try now to share my mistakes with others, to admit what I've got wrong and to be transparent in my thinking and troubleshooting. Whether I've got on my parenting hat, my director's hat or my researcher's hat, I try to remember what Ron taught me and share aloud my mistakes, my thinking and my next steps. I try to encourage those I teach to do the same. In particular, I think it's important for newer, less experienced members of a team to know that their more seasoned colleagues do not always get things right first time. This helps to break down some of the hierarchies and barriers present in many workplaces and can create a supportive culture of learning together.

## Looking ahead

One of the gifts of the pandemic is that we have all had to completely reimagine the way in which we do things. We've all had to be bold and brave and we've probably all made some mistakes along the way. My commitment to myself is never to get less bold and brave in my learning and doing than the pandemic has forced me to be, but to always try to hold my hands up when I get things wrong. To present my mistakes in such a way that bolsters the confidence of others and to always strive to create safe environments for the gifting of mistakes in any sessions that I'm leading or teaching in future.

This has been especially hard online, but I look forward to the buzz of the room in face-to-face training sessions where I can see the relief on colleagues' faces as they unburden to each other about the things they've recently got wrong and they find new ways forwards together.

## ⬇ THINGS YOU COULD TRY

Here are some things you could try if you'd like to apply this lesson to your own life:

1. **Fail of the day** – as a family, class or group of colleagues, take a light-hearted look at what went wrong today and what could be learned from it.

   *Make a start by* noting down some recent fails and what you learned from them:

   1. ................................................................

   2. ................................................................

   3. ................................................................

2. **Make a habit of gifting your mistakes** – when you've learned a lesson the hard way, being brave enough to gift your mistakes and sharing with friends or colleagues where you went wrong so they don't have to is a real kindness.

   *Make a start by* noting down a mistake a colleague could learn from:

   ................................................................

   ................................................................

   ................................................................

Now find a moment to share this mistake so it can do its magic.

3. **Consider how you respond to other people's mistakes** – consider whether you're encouraging the people you work with or care for to share what goes wrong as well as what goes well. Often, we praise outcome rather than effort and little time is given over to joint problem-solving. If you'd like those around you to be more honest about what went wrong and to explore it together, think about what small steps could create a culture that enables that. Listening intently and considering what actions we praise is a great start.

# Part 2

# LESSONS IN SELF-ACCEPTANCE

# 'You' is the very best person you can be

*If we stop striving to be someone we're not, and we embrace the person we are, great things can start to happen.*

## What I got wrong in the past

Like many people, I've spent much of my life striving to be someone that I'm not. I vividly recall at university trying to shed my past skin and start again thinking that if I looked, spoke and acted a little differently I'd feel differently too. Later in life, I had a vision of myself as a certain type of parent. Inspired by others who seemed to wear, do and say all the right things. If I wore, said and did those things, perhaps I'd be a perfect parent too?

It's an easy enough trap to fall into, always aspiring to be and do better, or finding ourselves inspired by the endeavours of others and wondering if perhaps we can be a little bit more like them. Sometimes it's by trying to change the way we look, sometimes it's by trying to change the way we behave and sometimes it's about trying to change the way we feel.

But when we're constantly striving to be someone we're not, we're never comfortable in our own skin. We're like a child trying on a parent's shoes for size and clip-clopping around the place in the ill-fitting shoes of someone they admire. Children take the shoes off though, whereas as adults we sometimes persevere with trying to walk in others' treads no matter how ill the fit.

What if instead we allow ourselves simply to be? To discover the different facets of ourselves and celebrate everything big and small that makes us unique, then maybe life becomes more comfortable. No longer do we have to manage the cognitive load of trying to be someone else all day long and we can relax into simply being ourselves. It's a relief, it saves a lot of energy and with a little practice we'll find that being the person we were meant to be is easier, more comfortable and way more glorious than passing our lives being a pale imitation of someone we're not.

## The lesson and the teacher

To be honest, with a few notable exceptions, other people have generally always liked me more than I like myself. But I've only relatively recently been open to really learning this lesson. I'd spent so much of my life trying to be someone and something I wasn't, hiding from the traumas of my past, not accepting the limitations that autism placed on my present and beating myself up for all the things I couldn't do rather than celebrating what I could do and who I am.

But in more recent times, I've learned to see myself through the eyes of a very dear friend. On a difficult day recently when he'd held my hands through tears and panic as he has so often in the past (a friend who knows how to guide you through a panic attack is a friend indeed), I fell into my usual cycle of apologies and self-doubt. Arthur's response was 'You are perfect just as you are', which the Bridget Jones fans among you will appreciate. But the thing was, he meant it. He loves me warts and all and on the calmer days he helps me to see how my challenges make me stronger and that, without my issues past and present, my life would have taken quite a different shape and that would not necessarily be a wholly good thing.

When someone you really trust, and who really knows the depths of your insecurities and the origins of your trauma, thinks that you're okay, then maybe it's a sign that you are.

## What I do now

This is very much a lesson I'm still learning. There are a lot of reasons that I find it hard to love and truly be myself, not least that

I've not had much chance to get to know myself yet. I've spent so much of my life numbed and hiding behind anorexia and self-harm and doing what I needed to please others, to escape anger or simply to fit as an autistic person in a neurotypical world that I don't really know myself fully yet. But I'm starting to look forward to the idea of getting to know me and being a little more me.

## Looking ahead

I hope to give myself the space and time I need to grow and heal and to really find my feet and learn to be myself. I may not look or think or feel or behave exactly as I might have hoped to, but just as I love the diversity of the people I have the joy of inter-acting with every day, I look forward to embracing the diversity of my true character. I hope to allow myself to love, to live and to work in ways that are truer to myself and to demonstrate to my daughters as they approach adolescence that the very best person we can each be is ourselves.

## ⬇ THINGS YOU COULD TRY ▨▨▨▨▨

Here are some things you could try if you'd like to apply this lesson to your own life:

1. **Consider who your role models are** – are they the right kind of role models? Will they help you to be the truest version of yourself or will they encourage you to simply try to be somebody else entirely?

   *Make a start by* listing your role models and circling the ones that help you to be the truest version of yourself:

   1. ................................................................

   2. ................................................................

   3. ................................................................

   4. ................................................................

**5.** ...........................................................

**6.** ...........................................................

**7.** ...........................................................

**8.** ...........................................................

2. **Connect with what makes you you** – what are the things that are the very essence of you? When, where, doing what and with whom do you feel like the most authentic version of yourself? I find a helpful touch point here is thinking about times you laugh or cry hard and without embarrassment. The faces and spaces you're occupying when that happens can help you to connect with the true you.

   *Make a start by* writing about a time when you recently laughed or cried and why you felt safe to do so:

   ...........................................................
   ...........................................................
   ...........................................................
   ...........................................................

3. **Kick off those ill-fitting shoes** – are there any aspects of your life that feel like that ill-fitting pair of shoes? Are there any ways you're trying to look, act or feel that just aren't a snug fit with the real you? If so, can you kick off those shoes and find a more comfortable pair?

   *Make a start by* noting down aspects of your life that don't feel like a good fit:

   ...........................................................
   ...........................................................
   ...........................................................
   ...........................................................

# Being thinner is not a shortcut to happiness

There is no shortcut to happiness, and in particular being thinner or being stronger, which society teaches us will make us happier, will not do so.

## What I got wrong in the past

This is a biggie for me as I have a long history of anorexia. While my relationship with food and weight and exercise is long and complicated, somewhere within that whole mess of a relationship is a feeling that things will be different if only I can eat less and weigh less and take up less space.

I'm far from an endpoint in this journey but I think I'm closer than I have been in the past, and while I still need to think carefully about my relationship with food and exercise every day, one lesson I categorically know is that being thinner does not make me happier. Far from it. In my thirties, I suffered a massive anorexia relapse which saw me hospitalized for months and on round the clock suicide watch. I was so thin that I was at risk of death. Was I happy? Erm, no. Not even a little bit. There were moments of respite – happy times when people would visit, the cuddles from my daughters, the songs my husband Tom recorded for me every night – but those glimpses of happiness were glimpses of a life beyond my hospital bed, the life I had starved my way away from.

## The lesson and the teacher

When I was in hospital I had a wonderful nurse, Inke, who would sit with me for hours every day and often through the night as well. She was never judgemental and never made me feel that my illness was my fault or that I should just get over it or any of those things. But she did often reflect on how many wonderful people I had in my life. She marvelled at the frequency and variety of different visitors I had and the cards and flowers which people were so kind in sending. I remember one day her saying, 'You have a life full of love, let's get you well enough to live it.' I'm sure that she and other members of my care team, as well as my friends, family and colleagues, must have said similar words to me many times but on that day I was ready. I was ready to walk away from the half-life that is anorexia and to fully commit to being well. It wasn't easy then and years later it's still not. But things are changing. These recent years are the first in which I've worked hard to fight the urge to give in to starving or purging or exercising to excess, the first when I've allowed my body to find it's natural size and to sit with it, and they are also the first time I've experienced genuine, uncomplicated joy.

## What I do now

I'm heavier now, and healthier and happier. I'm not sure I'll ever feel happy with the way I look but I have a newfound respect for my body which has birthed babies, run a marathon, survived abuse and not given up, even when it could have, and has now grown strong with my new love of climbing. It's littered with self-harm scars and there are wobbly bits I dislike and overly muscly bits which are not the best either, but you know what, it's a pretty cool body really and it's the only one I've got. I'm about double the weight I once was, and my life is certainly better and happier for me and those I love, now that I'm no longer emaciated and at danger of shutting down and dying.

Every now and then I despair at how much space I take up, but I give myself a talking to and remind myself of how very much there is to lose alongside the 'few pounds' I find myself contemplating. I've never felt sadder, more desperate or more as if I was taking up too much space than when I was at my very thinnest. I'll take a few extra pounds and a side helping of healthy and happy please.

## Looking ahead

As well as trying to stay happy and healthy myself, I have a key challenge ahead to help my daughters navigate adolescence and beyond in a world that is obsessed with telling them how they should look, think and feel. My girls are just beautiful inside and out and my number one job now is to demonstrate to them an acceptance of self; to avoid negative talk of diet and weight; to help them marvel at the amazing things their bodies can do when they tear them away from a screen. I hope to help them believe that short or tall, fat or thin they are my brilliant girls. Of course, I can tell my girls until I'm blue in the face and they won't hear it...but if I *show* them, then maybe, just maybe, they can avoid the challenges I've faced due to assuming happiness is linked to shape and weight.

## THINGS YOU COULD TRY

Here are some things you could try if you'd like to apply this lesson to your own life:

1. **Think back to a time when you laughed out loud with friends** – bring it right to mind and remember how it felt. I'll bet that the feelings that flood your body are all about who you were with, what was going on, what was sparking such joy? I bet you can't remember at all what anyone was wearing and whether they were looking fatter or thinner than usual? Remember this next time you find yourself wondering about shedding a few pounds or gaining some muscle in order to boost your self-esteem.

2. **Curate your social media feeds** – especially on image-sharing sites. Try to cleanse your feed so that there is more emphasis on things that make you happy and less emphasis on the things that make advertisers happy. Unfollow brands or influencers which tap into your insecurities about your appearance and follow people who are passionate about topics you care deeply about, or who make you laugh out loud.

3. **If it doesn't fit, get rid of it** – I'll talk more about this later, but one of the sticks with which we often beat ourselves is that favourite old pair of skinny jeans or that dress that used to fit but doesn't do up anymore. Keeping these old friends hanging around in our wardrobe is a constant reminder that we've changed shape in a way that we feel a little unhappy with and we can be tempted to think, 'If only I was that size again, things would feel better.' They wouldn't. Happiness is more than jeans-size deep.

# Learn what others love about you

Sometimes it can feel hard to find things to love about ourselves, but if we turn to the people around us, we'll often find they're brimming with ideas.

## What I got wrong in the past

I spent a lot of time in the past judging myself by my own standards and never giving myself a break. I compared my failures with other people's triumphs and I was always fast to zoom straight in on my flaws and imperfections. When viewed through my own eyes, I was ugly inside and out and certainly not a person worthy of the love, friendship or respect of others, yet I found myself always surrounded by brilliant people. People who were kind and caring and who I respected and admired. Somehow this exacerbated the problem and left me feeling constantly unworthy of the amazing company I kept.

It was uncomfortable to say the least.

## The lesson and the teacher

After a while, I started to become aware of friends who viewed themselves very differently from how I viewed them and I would find myself wishing that if only for a day they might be able to see themselves through the same lens that I used. I began to wonder if maybe this was true of myself as well.

Especially if you struggle with the whole self-love thing, it can be pretty challenging to objectively list the things about yourself which are, well, lovable. But if you're able to take a step back and view yourself through not your own eyes but the eyes of others, it can help you recalibrate a little.

While many people over the years have been kind enough to share with me the things that they find valuable about my life and work, the people from whom I've learned the most are my daughters, Lyra and Ellie.

Parenting is an area of huge insecurity for me, and I always feel that while I'm able to give good advice to other parents, and I know the 'theory' well, I find it hard to be the parent I want to be. I'm guilty of comparing my parenting to others' via social media, and while I know, I *know*, that they are sharing carefully curated highlights, I still find myself coming up short.

But when I talk to my children about my parenting and that of my husband (who is, to be fair, the best dad in the world), they speak very positively indeed. Of course, there are things they wish we'd do differently, McDonald's every night and unlimited screen time among them, but on the whole they are full of love and questions rather than anything other. My girls tell me that they know they are loved, they tell us they can talk to us about anything and they know that if something goes wrong, no matter what it is, we'll help them. And their actions suggest these things to be true.

Especially during these times of pandemic, when we've had to try and ensure that there is some kind of business left after all the lockdowns and when home schooling at the same time as running a business and carrying out building work all felt like rather too much at times, it seems that as a family we've grown stronger. We've not been on fancy holidays, but we play a mean game of Dobble and our debates over the dinner table are getting more interesting by the week. There's nothing quite like a couple of headstrong nearly teens and a headstrong granny alongside Mum and Dad to ensure that the conversation never lulls.

## What I do now

My therapist used to often ask me 'What is the evidence for that?' when I stated an opinion as if it were fact. I try to ask this question when evaluating myself these days, and instead of assuming that my internal negative narrative is true, I proactively look for external evidence to the contrary. Am I perfect? Hell no, but do other people's opinions of me differ from my own? Well, that's a great big yes. So I try to give weight to the opinions of those I love and trust and try (though it's hard) to silence the doubts that circle within, always.

## Looking ahead

As well as acknowledging that my view of myself is at odds with the view of those I trust and respect, I'm hoping to lean into the things that other people tell me they like about me. I am sometimes surprised by the things that people value or like about me. Often, they are things that would never have occurred to me. I'd like to lean into those things and do them even more, so long as they're things that align with my personal values and vision.

## THINGS YOU COULD TRY

Here are some things you could try if you'd like to apply this lesson to your own life:

1. **Talk to your friends about the things you most value about them** – you'll likely find that they're surprised and that they view themselves very differently from the way you do.

   *Make a start by* noting down the things you value most about some of your friends:

   . . . . . . . . . . . . . . . . . . . . . . . . . . . . . . . . . . . . . . . . . . . . . . . . . . . . . . . . . . . . . . . . . . . . . . . .

   . . . . . . . . . . . . . . . . . . . . . . . . . . . . . . . . . . . . . . . . . . . . . . . . . . . . . . . . . . . . . . . . . . . . . . . .

   . . . . . . . . . . . . . . . . . . . . . . . . . . . . . . . . . . . . . . . . . . . . . . . . . . . . . . . . . . . . . . . . . . . . . . . .

Your next step is to share these things with those they pertain to.

2. **Be brave and ask them to reciprocate** – this can feel a little awkward, but it's so worthwhile. If you feel down about yourself, opening up to a friend or colleague whose opinion you value, sharing a little of your insecurities and asking if their opinion chimes with or differs from yours can be humbling and magnificent. If it's too hard to have this as a verbal conversation, writing it down and emailing or texting can work well. You'll also then have the response in writing so you can refer back to it any time you need a boost.

   *Make a start by* talking to your friends and noting down the things they say they value about you:

   . . . . . . . . . . . . . . . . . . . . . . . . . . . . . . . . . . . . . . . . . . . . . . . . . . . . . . . . .

   . . . . . . . . . . . . . . . . . . . . . . . . . . . . . . . . . . . . . . . . . . . . . . . . . . . . . . . . .

   . . . . . . . . . . . . . . . . . . . . . . . . . . . . . . . . . . . . . . . . . . . . . . . . . . . . . . . . .

   . . . . . . . . . . . . . . . . . . . . . . . . . . . . . . . . . . . . . . . . . . . . . . . . . . . . . . . . .

   . . . . . . . . . . . . . . . . . . . . . . . . . . . . . . . . . . . . . . . . . . . . . . . . . . . . . . . . .

   . . . . . . . . . . . . . . . . . . . . . . . . . . . . . . . . . . . . . . . . . . . . . . . . . . . . . . . . .

   What surprised you?

   . . . . . . . . . . . . . . . . . . . . . . . . . . . . . . . . . . . . . . . . . . . . . . . . . . . . . . . . .

   . . . . . . . . . . . . . . . . . . . . . . . . . . . . . . . . . . . . . . . . . . . . . . . . . . . . . . . . .

   . . . . . . . . . . . . . . . . . . . . . . . . . . . . . . . . . . . . . . . . . . . . . . . . . . . . . . . . .

   . . . . . . . . . . . . . . . . . . . . . . . . . . . . . . . . . . . . . . . . . . . . . . . . . . . . . . . . .

3. **Question your negative self-narrative** – any time you find your internal dialogue doing you down, ask yourself, 'Where's the evidence for that?', or even better, see if you can find evidence for an alternative point of view.

*Make a start by* noting down a negative thought or self-view that occurs often and writing down the evidence for a different stance:

. . . . . . . . . . . . . . . . . . . . . . . . . . . . . . . . . . . . . . . . . . . . . . . . . . . . . . . . . . . .

. . . . . . . . . . . . . . . . . . . . . . . . . . . . . . . . . . . . . . . . . . . . . . . . . . . . . . . . . . . .

. . . . . . . . . . . . . . . . . . . . . . . . . . . . . . . . . . . . . . . . . . . . . . . . . . . . . . . . . . . .

. . . . . . . . . . . . . . . . . . . . . . . . . . . . . . . . . . . . . . . . . . . . . . . . . . . . . . . . . . . .

# There is nothing more credible than authenticity

Being authentic, honest and vulnerable about your struggles will not necessarily harm your credibility. Sometimes it will even enhance it.

## What I got wrong in the past

I spent the first few years of my career hiding my own challenges and teaching from a completely theoretical standpoint. I was teaching about topics I knew well, in particular eating disorders and self-harm, but at no point did I open up to those I was teaching that these were current struggles in my life. I might sometimes have alluded to past experiences; somehow that felt palatable – to be able to intimate that I used to struggle with those things but 'I'm recovered now' felt like an appropriate story to tell.

The thing is, that wasn't the truth. Those things were still very much present in my life. Sometimes I was kind of managing them, but then came the big crash in my thirties that saw everything fall apart and there were years of mental and physical instability while I battled with my inner demons.

One day I remember vividly, I was giving a lecture to a couple of hundred psychiatrists about the latest advances in eating disorder understanding and treatment. It was a session that was really well received and many of those attending asked me to join them for lunch to explore the ideas further. There were a lot of things I could do, but lunch with people I didn't know with food I had no control over wasn't one of them. It was so far from something I could do that I made my excuses and left very abruptly, finding myself walking through central London in a daze thinking to myself, 'But this is great, if I wander a while, everyone will think I ate at the conference and I can get away without eating lunch.'

I stopped in my tracks, noticing this thought and realizing that I was living a lie. I was teaching about the very thing that was plaguing me. But I didn't know how to stop it, and to be honest, at that point, I didn't want to. So I didn't.

You don't have to fast forward too far to find me seriously unwell with anorexia as well as its common bedfellows for me of anxiety, depression, suicidality and self-harm. But I didn't talk to anyone; I worked really hard to hide what was going on. It was only when I blacked out in the bathroom one morning and, as I had hidden my body from him for weeks, my husband got a real shock at the weight I'd lost that things came to a head.

But still I didn't talk about it. Not really. To a few people, yes, I had to – you can't take time off work for illness and treatment without your boss knowing and of course one or two people close to me noticed, though you'd be amazed at just how many people don't see what they don't want to, or what they don't think to look for. Or how many people cling on to silence and uncertainty even if they are worried. But I didn't make it easy for people to broach the subject because I put on the 'I'm fine' mask and I carried on with my everyday life.

How could I do anything other? I would surely lose all my credibility if I opened up about my own struggles, and besides, who would care?

## The lesson and the teacher

There was a lot of silent struggling before this lesson was finally learned. It was one of my best friends, Joe, who held me to account on this one. His remembering and mine of this conversation differ. I think in black and white whereas he's all about the shades of grey, so you'll have to imagine a little more love and care woven into this interaction, because with Joe there is always a lot of love and care. But the bits of the conversation I heard and took away with me were that I had to do better. That I was a role model and that I was giving people something unrealistic to aspire to. That by being in a relatively prominent and influential position in the world of mental health and yet pretending everything was fine, I was not leading well. That by being more authentic, more honest, more me, I would be being a better role model.

He was right. I was terrified.

Lying in my hospital bed too thin and weak even to sit up and with arms that told stories of managing only by hurting myself, I remember saying to Joe that I couldn't possibly share this messed up truth. I literally wrote the book on self-harm and eating disorders, and yet I couldn't manage those problems in myself. I'd surely lose all authority. He told me he thought I was wrong, and that it was the fact that I was fighting and would overcome these demons myself that made my story powerful and that this would lend me more, not less, credibility.

And so, slowly at first, I began to tell a more authentic version of my journey. I shared the downs as well as the ups and I trusted that people would see beyond the brokenness of now and would walk with me. I was instantly enveloped in love, by all but a notable few. The majority of people walked right alongside me through my darkest months and they still traverse the peaks and troughs with me now.

And did it harm my credibility? Not one jot. If anything it seemed to lend me more authority and I occasionally have to pull people up for referring to me as an expert by experience on occasions when I feel that my PhD and many years of research and work in the field are what underpin my expertise rather than having walked the walk. Certainly, the two things together are a powerful combination which have enabled me to have a meaningful and lasting impact on some really exciting projects over the years.

## What I do now

I try really hard to be honest about the ups and downs of my mental health, to paint a more realistic picture of living life with mental illness than is often portrayed. I use the term 'living experience' where most use 'lived experience' because for me mental illness is a part of my day-to-day. And I say that not in a defeatist way but rather in a realistic way. If I'm not vigilant, anorexia could take grip again, and anxiety and depression loom large fairly often. The post-traumatic stress disorder and autism which underpin it all are also things I live with every day, with more success on some days than others.

I think it's important that people have role models to look up to who don't show an idealized version of recovery. I certainly find that awareness days, and, in particular, Eating Disorders Awareness Week, are full of people's perfect stories and I cannot help but compare myself and find myself wanting. So I tend not to look anymore. I largely check out from social media during those weeks but share, 52 weeks a year, a slightly more real version of me, trying my hardest, mostly managing. Sometimes not.

## Looking ahead

I hope that the version of me I share with the world is a better and more realistic role model than the one that Joe pulled me up on all those years ago. I work hard to keep it real while also taking care not to become defined only by my struggles. I focus too on the things that bring me joy and pride and make me happy. I talk about my hobbies and interests and family and friends and celebrate the bits that are going well. But if it's a down day, I try to find the courage to be honest about it. I share the doubts and questions I have with the world, and I ask for help and encouragement. Miranda, a colleague and friend, who has great influence in the field of mental health, recently told me that I had been instrumental in helping to change the conversation around living with mental illness, especially for those working in the field. I'm immensely proud of that, but there is much more to do and it's not a job for me, it's a job for all of us. By sharing and supporting and finding our way through life together, no matter how messy it might sometimes get, we can help to change the conversation.

## ⬇ THINGS YOU COULD TRY

Here are some things you could try if you'd like to apply this lesson to your own life:

1. **Consider if there are bits of yourself that you choose not to share** – if so what are they and what's your reason for keeping shtum? Do you think it would help you or others if you were to be a little more open?

   *Make a start by* identifying those quiet but important parts of your character or experience:

   . . . . . . . . . . . . . . . . . . . . . . . . . . . . . . . . . . . . . . . . . . . . . . . . . . . . . . . . .

   . . . . . . . . . . . . . . . . . . . . . . . . . . . . . . . . . . . . . . . . . . . . . . . . . . . . . . . . .

   . . . . . . . . . . . . . . . . . . . . . . . . . . . . . . . . . . . . . . . . . . . . . . . . . . . . . . . . .

   . . . . . . . . . . . . . . . . . . . . . . . . . . . . . . . . . . . . . . . . . . . . . . . . . . . . . . . . .

   Make a note of a person you could speak to or a place where you'd feel safe talking about or exploring these parts of you:

   . . . . . . . . . . . . . . . . . . . . . . . . . . . . . . . . . . . . . . . . . . . . . . . . . . . . . . . . .

   . . . . . . . . . . . . . . . . . . . . . . . . . . . . . . . . . . . . . . . . . . . . . . . . . . . . . . . . .

   . . . . . . . . . . . . . . . . . . . . . . . . . . . . . . . . . . . . . . . . . . . . . . . . . . . . . . . . .

   . . . . . . . . . . . . . . . . . . . . . . . . . . . . . . . . . . . . . . . . . . . . . . . . . . . . . . . . .

2. **Openly show your support and encouragement of friends and colleagues who share** – it takes a huge amount of courage to be open and honest about challenging aspects of our

lives. When someone you love or respect does so, don't let it pass without comment.

*Make a start by* identifying a friend or colleague whose honesty you admire; then reach out and let them know:

. . . . . . . . . . . . . . . . . . . . . . . . . . . . . . . . . . . . . . . . . . . . . . . . . . . . . . . .

. . . . . . . . . . . . . . . . . . . . . . . . . . . . . . . . . . . . . . . . . . . . . . . . . . . . . . . .

3. **Look for role models who share some of your challenges** – if there are parts of your own life that you find difficult or challenging or which differ from the experience of those around you, look online for authentic influencers sharing their journey and experiences with similar issues. Where you find an authentic influencer, you'll likely find a whole tribe of followers ready to see you when you're ready to be seen.

   *Make a start by* identifying authentic influencers to follow, or people to ask for suggestions:

   1. . . . . . . . . . . . . . . . . . . . . . . . . . . . . . . . . . . . . . . . . . . . . . . . . . . . . .

   2. . . . . . . . . . . . . . . . . . . . . . . . . . . . . . . . . . . . . . . . . . . . . . . . . . . . . .

   3. . . . . . . . . . . . . . . . . . . . . . . . . . . . . . . . . . . . . . . . . . . . . . . . . . . . . .

# This feeling will pass

Sometimes things feel so bad that it seems almost impossible to carry on. But if you do, things begin to feel just a little bit easier.

## What I got wrong in the past

No matter how many times you have a panic attack, it feels like you're dying. This is something that I've spoken to many fellow sufferers about and it seems to be a pretty universal feeling. No matter whether it's your first or your thousandth, it feels as if this is the one you can't survive. You feel the world closing in on you, your heart exploding, your lungs short of breath and your brain shutting down, able to sustain panic but not thought, actions or words, and you give up. Or at least, that's how it's often felt for me.

I would often get lost in my panic, pushing away the things and people that might help and sinking into the misery of that feeling of the world ending. For me, historically, this panic and depth of despair would often lead to incidents of self-harm and occasionally to attempts at suicide. The one saving grace for me was that I kept my home safe (locking away sharp objects and medicines) and these depths usually occurred when I was too anxious to even contemplate leaving the house – something that could last weeks on end.

## The lesson and the teacher

All big feelings pass with time; our bodies and brains simply aren't able to sustain the complete extremes of anxiety (or indeed joy) for great long periods of time. It's physically and mentally exhausting and, after a while, the body and brain will start to meander back a little closer to normal functioning. If you're able to find a safe way to wait, things do get better. Nothing needs to fundamentally change; whatever triggered the anxiety doesn't need to change and go away; it just begins to feel a little bit better.

I know this. I teach about it. I occasionally even show fancy graphs about the extinction effect, but like so much of my teaching, it took me years to apply the lessons I taught to my own life. It was my friend Lucas who first helped me to really apply this idea to myself and to understand that no matter how hard the feeling, it would pass. Ironically, he repeated my own words and teaching back to me. I fell into a spiral of panic and anxiety as we sat in a pub after a day when we'd been teaching together, and he gently reminded me of my own words, of the things I'd taught that day about anxiety and panic and how to manage these moments.

He reassured me gently, kindly, and without judgement, that I wasn't going to die, that I was safe there with him, that he wasn't going anywhere and that the feeling would pass. He probably told me a dozen times before I began to actually hear him. But hear him I did and he was right. I didn't need to do anything except sit tight and trust in the universe in order for this feeling to become bearable again. After a little time, my thinking, speaking brain was calm enough to be functional, and with Lucas's help I was able to work out what to do next to get myself back on an even keel.

This came at a time when the cycle of panic and self-harm was pretty destructive in my life. Self-harm had felt like the only way to quell the panic. But that day, Lucas helped me to break the cycle and showed me that feelings, even really big, really scary ones, do pass, if only you can be patient.

## What I do now

The idea that 'this too shall pass' is true not just of panic but also of despair and grief and other challenging feelings too. If we can only find faces and spaces that help us to feel grounded and safe, we can work our way through almost anything given a little time. No feeling is so big and so unmanageable that it will last forever.

I like to envisage big feelings as being like a fire and my actions as things that can either starve or fan the flames. The things that starve the oxygen tend to be safety, calm, and slow, steady actions, self-care, self-love and putting myself in the path of those who care. I've found this helps too when faced with the distress of others. Being steady, safe and soothing and just allowing the person to sit with the feeling until it passes is more effective than any kind of deeper problem-solving I've tried.

I've trained myself now to respond better to moments when my anxiety peaks. I know that I can and will get through this time. I have prompts on my phone for these moments which remind me to sit with the feeling and to call a friend. Often the voice or the handhold of a friend can help those moments to pass more quickly. It's meant accepting myself as I am and trusting those I love to see me and help me in those moments of despair, which was hard at first as I used to do my hurting in private. But therein lay the path to self-harm. Now, I'm more open, more honest and I trust that this feeling will pass. And it has done every single time.

## Looking ahead

These moments are the moments that I find hardest to share. Maybe being a little more open and honest about them is the next step on that path to authenticity. I'm not sure. While there are people who know and who help, I do sometimes still find myself in situations where I'm inwardly panicking and doing everything I possibly can to hide it.

I'm the queen of the silent panic attack. Once I amazed an

anaesthetist who took my vitals and could not believe how calm I appeared, while my blood pressure and heart rate were through the roof. This is something of a survival mechanism for me and has meant I've been able to pass as 'normal' and continue with work and life even when I feel as if I'm dying inside. But ultimately, it's not actually healthy or helpful. In future, I'd like to learn to be more honest about how I'm actually feeling; to educate more people about how to help those who are struggling and to break down the stigma that still surrounds anxiety, panic and so much related to mental health.

When I work to hide my anxiety, and silently suffer with those panic attacks, the anxiety has to go somewhere. If it's not let out, it builds within and it's very, very toxic. And no, I don't want to do messy crying all over the place all the time or ask everyone to drop everything and sit with me as my feelings pass, but maybe I can get braver, and encourage others to get braver too, in asking to adapt situations that are likely to trigger panic and anxiety. And maybe I can learn to opt out as these feelings start to unfurl within me. Maybe I can have the confidence to take a step outside and look at the clouds or phone a friend before that gentle unfurling of anxiety takes a firm stranglehold. With practice, we can all learn to recognize those early warning signs that our anxiety is building and with a little confidence we can take steps to help the anxiety pass. It passes more quickly and fully if you catch it early.

I'm working on it.

## THINGS YOU COULD TRY

Here are some things you could try if you'd like to apply this lesson to your own life:

1. **Identify faces and spaces that make you feel safe** – think about where and to whom you can go when things feel most difficult. Wonder, too, if you can be this person for someone who trusts you.

*Make a start by* listing safe spaces and faces:

1. . . . . . . . . . . . . . . . . . . . . . . . . . . . . . . . . . . . . . . . . . . . . . . . . . .

2. . . . . . . . . . . . . . . . . . . . . . . . . . . . . . . . . . . . . . . . . . . . . . . . . . .

3. . . . . . . . . . . . . . . . . . . . . . . . . . . . . . . . . . . . . . . . . . . . . . . . . . .

4. . . . . . . . . . . . . . . . . . . . . . . . . . . . . . . . . . . . . . . . . . . . . . . . . . .

5. . . . . . . . . . . . . . . . . . . . . . . . . . . . . . . . . . . . . . . . . . . . . . . . . . .

2. **Work out the words that help you** – maybe you need to be reminded that this feeling will pass, that you're safe, that you're not alone...or maybe there are different words that help you. Trial, error and a little soul searching will help you discover what helps. I find it useful to carry these words with me either in writing or as a recording. You could also share these words with trusted friends so that they know what to say in difficult moments.

*Make a start by* noting down words or phrases that you find reassuring:

1. . . . . . . . . . . . . . . . . . . . . . . . . . . . . . . . . . . . . . . . . . . . . . . . . . .

2. . . . . . . . . . . . . . . . . . . . . . . . . . . . . . . . . . . . . . . . . . . . . . . . . . .

3. . . . . . . . . . . . . . . . . . . . . . . . . . . . . . . . . . . . . . . . . . . . . . . . . . .

3. **Learn your early warning signs** – following moments of high anxiety or panic, be curious about what the early warning signs were that you could have picked up on. Notice these over time so you can start to pick up on them earlier. It's far easier to manage panic before it peaks, so becoming familiar with the signs that you're starting to struggle can really help. Everyone is different but this might feel like a shortness of breath, sweating, dizziness, a loss for words, a feeling of falling, nausea or head pounding...you may have others too. Try to understand what your warning signs are and use this knowledge to help you to help yourself sooner rather than later.

*Make a start by* listing your early warning signs:

1. ................................................................

2. ................................................................

3. ................................................................

4. ................................................................

5. ................................................................

# Your childhood does not have to dictate your adulthood

You can strive to be anything and anyone. You do not have to be dictated to by the past and it is possible to break intergenerational cycles of harm or despair.

## What I got wrong in the past

It can be easy to assume that our futures are dictated by our past. Every parent feels the weight of responsibility when rearing their children knowing that we are setting them on a path for life. And while for those who are fortunate enough to have a positive start in life this early input is crucial and can indeed shape the adult they grow into, it doesn't have to be this way.

## The lesson and the teacher

I have a lot of feelings on this, but most of them aren't ones I feel quite ready to go into yet, but one example from my own early years that I particularly remember comes from the year after I'd finished school. I grew up in a seaside town and found myself working in a café in a children's theme park as I had done during many previous holidays from school. I loved it and I worked very hard, and although I had earned a place at university for the following year, I didn't really feel that I could or should take it. I felt that the café was where I fitted. I'd been accused by an adult I trusted of 'aiming above my station' with my ambitions for higher education and that accusation was one I heard loud and clear and deeply internalized.

I did my work in the café to the very best of my ability. You've never seen a cheese sandwich made with more love or care. But as time wore on, something niggled. I felt that maybe I could move away, maybe it wasn't my destiny to be always here. My life felt a little like *The Truman Show*, my job each evening was to ensure that things were left exactly as they'd started that morning. My last job each day was to erase any evidence of the hundreds of people who'd passed through our doors and to ready the café to start again tomorrow. Each day was the same, and after significant challenges in my earlier teens, I welcomed the structure, the routine and the fact that most of it could be done without much depth of thought.

When I'd been there a few months, Beryl retired. She was someone with whom I'd developed something of a friendship despite the decades that divided us. Beryl had worked at the theme park for longer than I'd been alive, and her retirement brought into sharp focus the future I was creating for myself readying the café each morning for its new guests and carefully erasing their existence that evening for years and years and years.

Beryl told me 'Just because the shoe fits doesn't mean you have to wear it' in that enigmatic way that older, wiser people have. But I knew just what she meant and I determined to take up my place at university, despite the fact that it was challenging and uncomfortable and I had no idea if I could make it work. Staying was the easy option. To leave, to start again, to make a new and different life was far harder. I'd love to say it was a fairy tale ending and that I loved every minute of my time at university. It wasn't and I didn't, but boy am I glad that I came to understand that there are different paths in life and that we don't always have to take the one that's clearly signposted and has been well trodden and predetermined.

## What I do now

In the intervening years, I've learned a lot more about neuroscience (thanks in part to my time at university, where dissecting human brains felt like a privilege and a highlight). I now know what I didn't then – that our brains are plastic and ever changing. While the neural pathways in our brains are more easily mapped and built during our early years, it is never ever too late to make a change.

We can always learn new things. It takes time, practice and a whole heap of hard work, but new neural pathways can be built at any time. We can change the way we love and feel loved. We can change the way we respond to anger or sadness. We can learn to solve a Rubik's cube or to play the piano or almost anything that we put our mind to.

That doesn't mean it's easy but it's often very rewarding. The understanding that it is possible to learn new things and change how we think and feel, even as an adult, has been a revelation to me. Though it sometimes feels that way, it is not true that the only option is to do things in the way they've always been done.

We can choose how to love, how to parent, how to work, how to do anything. It's a big responsibility but it's a welcome one if it allows us to step outside the shadows of the past and look towards a brighter future.

## Looking ahead

We can aspire to do different things from those we learned from the generations that came before us. Neither our careers nor our relationships are predetermined by what has happened in the past. Of course, it is harder to do something different from that which has been handed through the generations, but difficult is not impossible.

It's not easy to choose a different path from the one you may feel programmed to follow, but with strength, courage and the support of others, it is possible. I'm determined to keep challenging the assumptions that my past makes my future and prove that there is always another way.

## ⊕ THINGS YOU COULD TRY

Here are some things you could try if you'd like to apply this lesson to your own life:

1. **Reflect on your childhood and cherry pick the good bits** – which are the bits you'd love to carry forward and pass down through the generations? Work hard not to lose these bits in the maelstrom of modern life.

   *Make a start by* listing the good bits you'd like to carry forwards:

   1. .........................................................
   2. .........................................................
   3. .........................................................
   4. .........................................................
   5. .........................................................

2. **Consider what you'd like to chuck** – as well as things you'd like to cherish, there are doubtlessly some parts of your childhood that you'd like to let go of. Give yourself permission not to perpetuate these cycles and to learn a different way of doing things.

   *Make a start by* listing the bits you'd like not to repeat:

   1. .........................................................
   2. .........................................................
   3. .........................................................
   4. .........................................................
   5. .........................................................

3. **Learn new things** – prove to yourself that you can change and that it's never too late to learn by having a go at something you've always had a hankering to learn to do. Perhaps you've always wondered if you could learn to juggle or make delicious chocolate brownies or perform the perfect slam dunk. Whatever it is, set yourself the challenge of trying and notice yourself learning. Be sure to enjoy the process and the laughs along the way.

   *Make a start by* writing about something you'd love to learn to do and the next step you could take towards doing the learning:

   . . . . . . . . . . . . . . . . . . . . . . . . . . . . . . . . . . . . . . . . . . . . . . . . . . . . . . . . . . . . . .

   . . . . . . . . . . . . . . . . . . . . . . . . . . . . . . . . . . . . . . . . . . . . . . . . . . . . . . . . . . . . . .

   . . . . . . . . . . . . . . . . . . . . . . . . . . . . . . . . . . . . . . . . . . . . . . . . . . . . . . . . . . . . . .

   . . . . . . . . . . . . . . . . . . . . . . . . . . . . . . . . . . . . . . . . . . . . . . . . . . . . . . . . . . . . . .

# You cannot control what others do, but you can control how you respond

There are some things we can control and some things we can't. Try as we might, we can't control what others do, but we can learn to manage the way in which we respond and react.

## What I got wrong in the past

When we experience challenge, the first place we look is often the source of the challenge and we find ourselves wondering if it can be changed. Of course, if the source of the challenge is someone else's words or behaviours, then that is often something that is very difficult to have an impact on, especially when those thoughts and actions are deeply entrenched and long held.

Like many people, in the past when the words and actions of others have distressed, worried or otherwise upset me, I've tried to change the source. I've tried to fix or change the person or change their point of view. I've rallied against the source of the torment, hoping it would change. Most often, this has exemplified itself as me trying to convince someone to like me who didn't. In particular, a friendship which formed rapidly and deeply in recent years, but which soured beyond belief for reasons I've never fully understood, left me trying, in vain, to change the opinion of the friend who'd fallen out with me.

Mental illness was what bound us together and it was, I think, what drove us apart. My friend had warned me at the start of our friendship that due to his personality disorder he found it hard to love and be loved and that he had a history of turning against the people who were kindest to him. I heard his words, but I didn't really hear him, choosing instead to lean into our friendship and to cherish the nice times we had together. But things did sour and, just as he'd warned me, the depths of his unkindness were shocking. He took what he knew about my insecurities and turned these things against me; his words and messages were pure poison. But we'd been really good friends and he'd warned me this might happen. I, perhaps like others before me, thought I could change him.

I couldn't. The more I tried to change his view of me, the deeper his anger, vitriol and unkindness grew. It made me sad, triggered my anxiety and made me feel unsafe and edgy any time I'd go near the places we'd often spent time together, always unsure if he might be around the corner.

## The lesson and the teacher

The lesson came from an unlikely source: Ian, someone who was acquainted with us both and had observed this pattern within our relationship, having seen it play out before. He told me something that I felt I should have known, but which the dark cloud of the current situation had prevented me from seeing. While I could not change how my friend treated me, I could change how I responded and whether or not I internalized his opinions of me and adopted them as my own. This is an easy trap to fall into when the unkindness of another takes the shape of the unkindness you've felt towards yourself in the past.

Picking myself up was hard, much harder than lying down and allowing myself to be beaten, but Ian was right. I decided that I would no longer internalize the words of my past friend, that I would allow them to wash off me and to know that they were simply his opinion and did not have to shape mine. I could not stop him saying and doing these things, but I could take measures to protect myself both physically and mentally.

He hated me. His hatred was deep and full. It hurt, a lot, but try as I might I couldn't seem to change how he felt about me or the way in which he was behaving. But I could, and did, change how I responded.

My new approach brought our friendship to a fairly rapid and quiet close. It sizzled out as we each moved on to pastures new. Does this friend still hate me? I don't know, I'll never know, but I hope not. It's okay if he does. How he feels is his business; how I respond is mine.


## What I do now

When other people hold entrenched opinions, I am at peace with the fact that there is often little I can do to change them. This might sound defeatist but I've learned that change happens far more rapidly and fully by engaging those who have some sympathy for the cause. For this reason, I've largely stepped away from my campaigning and lobbying roles which used to see me spend a lot of time in Westminster, trying to persuade people to change policy. I had some success but it was slow and hard won and often only happened when the desired policies aligned with a leader's current vision and was always subject to the winds of change. Instead, now I look to the many people with whom I share a vision and I think about how we can make a difference together.

Rather than trying to persuade politicians, I spend much of my time teaching those directly on the frontline. In my work I can make more difference to children by working with those who directly work with or care for them and who want to hear what I have to say than I can ever have by trying to persuade someone way up the pecking order who may or may not have an interest in our agenda.

I have huge admiration for friends and colleagues who continue to fight the big fights, but I've found that in both my personal and professional endeavours it is truly hard to change how people think and act. The lesson that I can decide whether to internalize that and rise above it has been an important one, but fundamentally my key learning here is that it's hard to force change on people.

## Looking ahead

I try to notice quickly when people are acting or speaking in ways that challenge or upset me. It's okay for many different viewpoints to exist in the world, but it's deeply uncomfortable to spend my days striving to change things that cannot be changed. I work hard not to take it personally when people see little value in my work or life and I remind myself often that they are entitled to their point of view, and I to mine. I do not have to give their point of view permission to drag me down. I can instead turn to more receptive people, keen for the kind of change I'm trying to effect, and know that together we can make great things happen.

 **THINGS YOU COULD TRY**

Here are some things you could try if you'd like to apply this lesson to your own life:

1. **Acknowledge any toxic influences in your life** – do you have people who play to your insecurities and make you feel down about yourself? Do they have a right to make you feel that way or are you able to build a shield around yourself or walk away?

   *Make a start by* listing any toxic influences in your life:

   1. . . . . . . . . . . . . . . . . . . . . . . . . . . . . . . . . . . . . . . . . . . . . . . . . . . . . . . . . . . . . . .

   2. . . . . . . . . . . . . . . . . . . . . . . . . . . . . . . . . . . . . . . . . . . . . . . . . . . . . . . . . . . . . . .

   3. . . . . . . . . . . . . . . . . . . . . . . . . . . . . . . . . . . . . . . . . . . . . . . . . . . . . . . . . . . . . . .

2. **Hold on to what you're proud of** – connecting with the things that you value about yourself and really hanging on to those

hard when confronted with the dissenting views of others can be very helpful. Write them down and remind yourself of them any time you find someone's negative view blocking out a more positive self-view.

*Make a start by* noting down things that you're proud of:

1. ...........................................................

2. ...........................................................

3. ...........................................................

4. ...........................................................

5. ...........................................................

3. **Put the energy to good use** – sometimes other people's feelings will stir big energetic feelings within us, like anger. Consider whether you can take that energy and funnel it into making change happen in a positive way. Making the most of those energy spikes and using them to make good happen rather than shouting into the wind of an oppressor can often be a far more satisfying and productive use of time and energy.

*Make a start by* noting down any toxic energy you're holding and consider a first step you could take to funnel this energy into change rather than anger:

...........................................................

...........................................................

...........................................................

# You are irreplaceable

No matter how broken you might feel, there is only one you. You are, we all are, irreplaceable.

## What I got wrong in the past

During my darkest days, I felt totally expendable. I felt that if I vanished from the Earth things would be better for everyone. I felt like a burden to my friends and family and found it hard to find reasons to stay alive.

## The lesson and the teacher

This lesson was an accidental one, and one taught to me by my good friend Joe, whom those of you who've followed me a while will know and love. You'll have heard this story too perhaps – the post-it note story – but this book would not be complete without it, so if you're sitting comfortably then I'll begin.

This story happened at a time when things were pretty dark and desperate for me. I was battling with anorexia, self-harm and frequent thoughts of suicide. With amazing support from my husband, my therapist and Joe, who was my boss at the time, I was managing to work. This was important to me as work has always formed a crucial part of my self-identity, and the routines and rhythms of working life helped me not to fall deeper into the hole in which I found myself.

One day though, I'd had enough. I could not manage anymore. I just couldn't do it. While suicide had been on my mind for a while, this day I had a plan. I'd decided what, when and how it would happen. I was committed. Looking back at myself now, I'd consider myself to have been a very high suicide risk that day. When it comes to suicide, the move from loose contemplation to precise planning is a big warning sign.

I was due to leave the office and travel across London to a meeting in Westminster. Without going into details of my plan (which is never helpful and can be triggering for other people), I had no intention of making it to my meeting.

Before I left, Joe asked to chat with me. We went into a meeting room and none of the words that were said stay with me. It was Joe, they will have been good words, but they're gone, and just two words remain with me. He wrote them down and handed them to me as I prepared to leave the office. In black biro on a pale yellow post-it note he'd written 'You're Irreplaceable'. It was not that I believed these words to be true that altered my plans that day and saw me arrive safely in Westminster, but rather that I believed that Joe believed those words to be true. And I trusted Joe and his opinion.

## What I do now

Was Joe right? Was I, am I, irreplaceable? Are you? The answer is yes, we all are. We might be a mishmash of good bits and less good bits and triumphs and challenges and things we'd rather change, but we are, each and every one of us, unique and the world would be different without us in it.

Joe's words that day did enough to keep me safe; to steer me away from my plan for suicide; to connect me with a world in which I felt a little more wanted and needed; and to keep me living and breathing just a little bit longer. Joe's words are true not just for me, but for everyone. We're all unique. We're all irreplaceable, and even when our life feels less than worthwhile, that opinion is only our own, and when we look to those around us we may find dissenting voices. We may find people who value and love us more than perhaps we can value and love ourselves today.

So what do I do now? I try to be a little kinder to myself, noticing the dings I make in the universe, no matter how small. I realize that I'm the only person who is good at being me, no matter how painful that might feel some days, and I encourage those I love and care for to appreciate themselves as irreplaceable people too.

## Looking ahead

My aim, and I hope it's an aim that others would share, is to move from a point of needing external validation to sitting more comfortably with myself. I am irreplaceable, it matters that other people believe it to be true whether they're my friends, family or colleagues. But I'd love one day to get to a place where I sit comfortably with myself and can see myself as someone who deserves to be alive without the need of reassurance from others.

Honestly, it feels like a lofty aim, but a girl has got to dream, right?

## ⬇ THINGS YOU COULD TRY

Here are some things you could try if you'd like to apply this lesson to your own life:

1. **Tell a loved one they are irreplaceable** – if this lesson made you think of someone you care about, tell them. We don't tell people the good stuff enough and many, many people walk through life riddled with insecurity. When you take a moment to tell someone that their existence matters to you, it will lift you both up.

   *Make a start by* noting down someone you believe is irreplaceable and why:

   . . . . . . . . . . . . . . . . . . . . . . . . . . . . . . . . . . . . . . . . . . . . . . . . . .

   . . . . . . . . . . . . . . . . . . . . . . . . . . . . . . . . . . . . . . . . . . . . . . . . . .

Your next step is to tell them.

2. **Write down and keep the good things** – if someone says something that resonates deeply with you, write it down and refer back to it any time you need a bit of a boost. Sometimes it's hard to convince ourselves of a different truth to our internal one, but the written words of someone we respect can help to set the internal record straight.

   *Make a start by* bookmarking this page and writing down the words of others that make you glow. Refer back to them any time you need to:

   1. .................................................................
   2. .................................................................
   3. .................................................................
   4. .................................................................
   5. .................................................................

3. **Make a list of things that make you uniquely you** – it's time for a little self-love. Stop, just for a moment, and think of the things that you do that are unique to you. They don't need to be big things, just a collection of little, almost incidental things that build up to create the rich tapestry of you. Keep the list, add to it, try to own it.

   *Make a start by* listing things you say, do or are that are very 'you'. Ask friends and family for suggestions if you struggle.

   1. .................................................................
   2. .................................................................
   3. .................................................................
   4. .................................................................
   5. .................................................................

6. ..........................................................

7. ..........................................................

8. ..........................................................

9. ..........................................................

10...........................................................

Part 3

# LESSONS IN SELF-CARE

# Wear what makes you glow

Life is too short for clothes that make you feel bad. Instead, wear clothes that fit your frame and put a smile on your face.

## What I got wrong in the past

As someone with a long history of anorexia, I have a complicated relationship with clothes. I'm prone to bouts of self-loathing and it's hard for me not to despair when I have to go up a size in jeans, nor to feel that pang of joy when the size goes down. I don't particularly like clothes, nor do I especially care about my size or appearance; but a feeling of taking up too much space has always been present in my life and somehow being smaller has been an aim for many of my years, both as a child and as an adult.

Years of therapy and working on recovery from my eating disorder, and the wider, deeper issues which sustain it, have meant that I've moved on intellectually. I'm able to objectively stop tying my self-worth to my clothes size, but the big mistake I'd made in the past was allowing that theoretical, objective knowledge to be constantly undermined by the clothes sitting in my wardrobe.

I've been many sizes, many of them I hope never to be again. They were not a sign of success but of near-death. But still the clothes from those times, those tiny sizes that had no right to exist in my healthy adult life, still hung from the rails in my wardrobe and were stacked up neatly in my drawers. And as kooky as it might sound, those clothes spoke to me every day. 'Remember how much better life was when you were tiny' say 'those jeans' and 'Imagine the emotional numbness that would come with fitting back into me' says 'that dress'.

They're just clothes. I don't even like clothes, and yet every day no matter how healthy and happy I was, I was confronted with clothes that didn't fit, that should never fit again but which lured me like a drug.

## The lesson and the teacher

This lesson comes with thanks to my therapist. We did a lot of work together over a pretty long time and I could fill a whole book just with the lessons he taught me. This is one of the most important and I think it holds true not just for those of us with eating disorders but for everyone.

Mat gave me permission to let go of the clothes that no longer made me feel good. He challenged me to empty my wardrobe and put back in it only the things that fitted me and felt good. It left me with very little, but that's okay. Now every time I reached for something to wear I was confronted not with lots of stories of the past and different weights and shapes I had been, but with clothes that fit and functioned for the person I was now.

For a time, I kept the clothes I removed in my garage in case I ever needed them again. Their voices were quieter, but I could still hear them, so I let them go completely and allowed them to find new homes and raise a little money by donating them to my local Mind charity shop.

It was a revelation. Honestly. It was so freeing, and I've often recommended this process to others.

## What I do now

I repeat this process regularly now. I love to send to new homes clothes that don't feel good or which no longer fit. Like many people, during the Covid lockdown, I went up a clothes size, I'm the largest I've ever been and, for the first time, I was able to just notice that I had changed size, remove from my wardrobe what didn't fit and order up a few staples in the new size.

This would have been agony in the past, but I've got better with practice. I've also got better at forcing myself to try on clothes that are borderline and make an active decision on them. If I don't love them, they go. It might sound wasteful but most people I know have rails of clothes which they rarely wear. I have fewer clothes and I wear them all the time, and while I might not rejoice at the form my body takes in them, they do not make me want to weep and that is progress indeed.

## Looking ahead

I carry out this process with my daughters, and both my husband and mother-in-law have joined in too. It seems that even those of us without deep insecurities about how we look are capable of beating ourselves up about our changing body shape that comes with age (and lockdown life). With my daughters, who are currently 11, this feels especially important and I also encourage Ellie to think carefully about which hand-me-downs she would like to keep from her taller sister. We've become very good at working out what we love and sending back or passing on what we don't. It's not perfect, but I think that every member of our household is just a little happier in their day-to-day clothes and that really does make a big difference because we spend all day wearing them.

I hope that I can continue to be kind to myself and not get hung up on sizes. I'm going to keep holding myself to account on this one and keep working on it, and when in doubt, I'll ask myself what I'd like to be role-modelling to my daughters – that is usually the very best of yardsticks to try and measure up against.

**THINGS YOU COULD TRY**

Here are some things you could try if you'd like to apply this lesson to your own life:

1. **Remove distressing clothes from your wardrobe** – go through your clothes one by one and pass on anything that doesn't fit or doesn't feel good. Give yourself permission to let go.

2. **Wear what feels good** – you don't have to wait for a special occasion to wear clothes you love. Wear them every day and consider it an act of self-love. They do no good to anyone hanging in a wardrobe and waiting for a few outings a year.

3. **Invest only in clothes that spark joy** – next time you find yourself buying clothes, stop and ask, 'Do I love it?... Do I feel good in it?', and only buy the unequivocal yeses. A wardrobe with fewer clothes but all of which feel good and spark a little happiness or comfort is a far better wardrobe than one busting at the seams with clothes ready to drag you down.

# Self-care can be as simple as a smear of lipstick

When we build little moments of self-care, self-nourishment and self-love into our daily routine, little things can make a big difference.

## What I got wrong in the past

As someone who spent a lot of time hating on myself, self-love and self-care were not concepts that came easily to me. For the longest time, I thought that in order to embrace these things I was going to have to make big sweeping changes in my life, to radically alter things and do things completely differently. But I learned that it can be smaller and simpler than that and that when it comes to self-care, the effect is cumulative.

## The lesson and the teacher

Another nurse was the teacher for me in this case. When I was in hospital, although I was confined to bed and often would not speak to anyone other than my nurses for long periods of time, Vicky encouraged me to get into the habit of looking after myself. At first I found this strange and futile. I wasn't going to be seeing anyone, what difference did it make if I'd washed my face and brushed my hair? Vicky taught me the importance of doing these things for myself as a little act of self-love. She also encouraged me to wear lipstick. Nothing could have been further from my mind. I'd not worn lipstick or really much makeup at all before and I was lying in a hospital bed most of the time and crying over food for much of the rest of it. Lipstick? Really?

But she went and bought me a lipstick and asked me to trust her. She asked me each day to put on a little lipstick as a 'wee act of kindness to yourself' and to think kind thoughts as I was doing it each day. I did as asked (you didn't mess with Vicky; the nurses who work on eating disorder units are made of stern stuff indeed, though they are also the softest, kindest and most caring people you'd hope to encounter). I was a bit nonplussed at first but she asked me to stick with it.

## What I do now

It's five years later and I've still stuck with it. I don't especially care for how makeup makes me look, but the small amount I put on every morning brings to mind my kind Scottish nurse and encourages me to be kind to myself for just a moment. Something as simple as a smear of lipstick, while I inwardly note that this is an act of self-care and kindness, has made a really big difference to me. Not to how I look, but to how I feel.

These little things that we do repeatedly make a big difference over time. Spending 30 seconds of a morning being kind to myself each day might not sound like a lot, but when you add it together over years and years and years, that's a whole lot of self-love. It's also nice that this starts my day and gets me off on a positive foot. It can also be a reassuring gesture in times of challenge. I pop on some lipstick, I tell myself I CAN do this, I think of Vicky and the battles we won over the dinner table, and I'm ready for anything.

## Looking ahead

Habits are hard to break, so I'm keen to build in some more good ones when it comes to self-care. I'm always wondering about how to make the moments that I spend every day a little bit less about pure function and more about reflection and self-care. I'm working on my daily routines around showering, teeth brushing and going to bed, and thinking about how to build more positive moments into my day-to-day life, because all those little moments add up to a whole lot more happiness if we let them.

## ⊕ THINGS YOU COULD TRY

Here are some things you could try if you'd like to apply this lesson to your own life:

1.  **Turn habits into happy moments in your day** – think about things you do every day and wonder how you could weave a little bit of kindness to yourself into each activity.

    *Make a start by* listing three things you do every day and considering how these daily habits could become small moments of joy or self-care:

    1. ............................................................
    2. ............................................................
    3. ............................................................

2.  **Reframe your actions to make them for yourself rather than others** – often when we do our makeup or fix our hair or choose what to wear, we're thinking about how we're perceived by the rest of the world. Explore what happens when you reframe these regular activities and do them just for you – just to make you feel good and as an act of self-love.

    *Make a start by* listing three things you do for others that you could be doing for yourself instead:

    1. ............................................................
    2. ............................................................
    3. ............................................................

3. **Let the difficult thoughts pass by** – with any habit or ritual we perform often, we can end up going into a sort of autopilot and this can mean that difficult thoughts surface. If you're not ready yet to drown these thoughts out with thoughts of kindness to yourself, simply notice these thoughts and let them pass on by. They mostly do unless we pay them attention.

# Sleep is the most important thing

Most things feel better after a good night's sleep, and yet we often put sleep at the bottom of our list of priorities. Perhaps it should sit right at the top.

## What I got wrong in the past

Sleep is a funny thing. It's a fundamental human need and yet it's something many of us willingly deprive ourselves of and it's the first thing we forfeit when we have stretching deadlines and too much to do. In fact, not only do we not prioritize sleep, we often actively praise those who seem to manage with very little sleep and we wear our late nights and early mornings like a badge of honour.

But sleep matters. A decent quantity and quality of sleep is the best shortcut to wellbeing and the quickest and most sure way of getting things back on track if they've gone awry.

## The lesson and the teacher

The teacher in this instance was Arianna Huffington and learned via her book *Thrive* rather than directly. My friend Miranda had gifted me the book during a challenging period saying she'd found it to be full of useful guiding principles about living well and she hoped I might find it similarly helpful.

The part of the book that most deeply resonated with me were the pages about sleep. Arianna was open and honest about the fact that sleep had been low on her priority list for many years but she and a friend decided to switch things around and do an experiment where they put sleep first on the list to see how things changed. With such busy working lives and constant expectations on them from colleagues and family, they had to literally block out the time to sleep and hold it precious in their diaries. Arianna worried that sleeping more and therefore spending fewer hours working or working out would be detrimental to her physical wellbeing and productivity but she found the opposite to be true.

Her words struck a nerve with me. Lack of sleep was something I'd forced myself to endure for years. If I was truly honest with myself it was probably a form of self-harm; but (like thinness) one for which I was often praised. I decided that if sleeping more could help Arianna Huffington to aim higher and feel happier, than maybe it would work for me too. And it did.

## What I do now

Keeping sleep at the top of my priority list is less easy than it might sound and old habits die hard, but I try really hard to continue to prioritize sleep, to see it as a good and restorative thing and to notice how I feel and how much less happy and productive and emotionally regulated I am on the days when I've simply not had enough.

I try to stick to a routine around sleep and waking and I've worked hard to make my bedroom a tranquil, calm space designed only for resting and recuperating. I talk in my teaching often about the importance of sleep and I try to follow my own advice. Any time I feel my mental health beginning to dip, sleep is my first port of call, either as an instant reset on a really tricky day, or by re-establishing healthy sleep routines to try to help me navigate life's dips and ditches.

## Looking ahead

Having denied myself sleep for years and now having moved towards a more healthy and functional relationship with sleep, my aspiration is to learn to love it. To cherish it. To happily put it as number one on my list of priorities. My next steps are thinking about how I can build a more calming and tranquil evening routine which will lend itself to sleep. This is harder than it might sound with work and children to contend with too. But as my girls get a little older and their bedtimes slip a little later, we've started thinking together as a family about how best we can enjoy our evenings in part together and in part apart, in a way that means everyone feels rested and ready for bed.

We don't always achieve this, but we're getting there. Part of this has involved looking backward and seeking inspirations from the brilliant evening routines we, like so many parents, had for our girls when they were very small and thinking which bits of those might make a positive reappearance at this point in our lives.

## ⊕ THINGS YOU COULD TRY

Here are some things you could try if you'd like to apply this lesson to your own life:

1. **Make a commitment to prioritizing sleep** – if it can work for Arianna Huffington, it can work for you. Until you decide that sleep is important and a worthy use of your time, it will always be chipped away at. Notice how well you function after more and less sleep by keeping a journal. The evidence is usually pretty compelling.

2. **Change the conversation around sleep** – this is a biggie, but let's all try together to stop praising those who sleep a little and work a lot and let's stop seeing sleep as a punishment (an early bedtime for a young child sends a very powerful message that sleep is a bad thing). It will take persistence and time, but we can change the way that sleep is perceived if we work at it.

3. **Sleep luxuriously** – make your bed, your bedroom and your nightwear feel inviting. This doesn't have to cost the earth, but a few small changes to make sure our bedroom is inviting of rest can make us much more eager to head to bed. My pro tips here are to always make your bed; it is the work of a moment and is so much more inviting to return to. I'd also advocate investing in nightwear you love, which is a joy to wear and a delightful form of self-care.

*Make a start by* listing simple changes you could make to where and how you sleep to make it feel more wonderful:

1. ............................................................

2. ............................................................

3. ............................................................

4. ............................................................

5. ............................................................

# Fun exercise is the best exercise

When we find a way to keep active that feels fun and builds connection with others, we get more from it and we're less likely to give up.

## What I got wrong in the past

Like sleep, exercise is something I've had to radically revise my relationship with in recent years. Like many people with a history of anorexia, I have a history of a very dysfunctional relationship with exercise which was yet another way to harm rather than nurture myself.

This was a challenge as I found that running fast and hard really helped to ease the anxiety I felt all the time. But I used running apps to compare my times and was constantly pushing myself harder and harder, always needing today to be a little bit faster than yesterday and beating myself up if I slipped a few seconds. All this while I was severely restricting my food intake. I would literally run to the point of collapse, usually in the early hours of the morning so it would go unnoticed. Each time I'd come to, my first thought would be to get up and keep on running.

I was not well and to this day I've not been able to trust myself to take up running safely. Nor can I wear a pedometer or a Fitbit and I have to disable the step count on my phone as this is a number I've become obsessed with in the past.

I have a long and chequered history with running, and when I realized that I probably needed to just not do it anymore, I was uncertain as to how to exercise in a way that had a more positive impact on my life.

## The lesson and the teacher

I always joke that I went from being bed bound, to using a wheel-chair to using crutches to climbing – a natural progression – but that really was broadly what happened. A few months after I was discharged from hospital and while I was still regaining mass and strength, I took my children to Craggy Island bouldering centre. They had been there for a party and really wanted to go back. I'd booked them on for a taster session and Chris, the staff member who was taking the session, said that if I joined them and learned how to keep my children safe while climbing then in future I could supervise them myself rather than always having to book a staff member to do so.

So, having not intended to climb at all, I donned a pair of the centre's climbing shoes and joined my girls. We had a great time, though I do recall my hands feeling so tired at the end of that first session that I could barely grip the pen I needed to sign the waiver form for future sessions. Chris suggested that I come along to the ladies climbing sessions on a Tuesday as it would be a great way to get started and meet other people at Craggy. I did, and the rest is history. My whole family at Craggy have been just amazing in supporting me through highs and lows (no pun intended) and I have found a way of exercising that stretches and challenges me both physically and mentally and which is also a huge amount of fun. I quickly made climbing friends and together we climb, we fall, we succeed, we fail, and all with a smile on our faces and getting a little stronger each time.

Having people to climb with and the excitement of ever-changing routes to climb has meant that since I first started a few years ago now, my love of climbing has never waned. In fact, I've since learned to climb with ropes, become a qualified climbing instructor and done a little climbing in Spain and Slovenia and on England's South Coast. I also went on to lead the ladies climbing session which was my initial initiation and found great joy in supporting those new to climbing to get stuck in, to challenge themselves and to learn new techniques and build up their strength.

## What I do now

The lockdowns during the pandemic made me really appreciate how important a part of my wellbeing toolkit climbing had become, because it was gone and I struggled. One of the really challenging things was the return to climbing after each lockdown; with months of no climbing and little other activity, I returned with a lot less strength and was unable to climb routes I'd have managed easily before.

I'm actually really proud of how I tackled this problem with a little help from Craggy's centre manager Gareth, who told me to forget the grades (which tell you how hard a climb is) and just enjoy every climb. I don't think I'd really realized consciously that before the pandemic hit, while I was hugely enjoying my climbing, I'd found myself working towards harder and harder grades. I have always been driven to aim higher in all that I do. But since I've returned, I've totally revised how I climb. I try everything – easy stuff, hard stuff, middle of the road stuff, if it's set I'll try it and have fun trying. This new approach has meant that instead of beating myself up for what I can't do yet, I just lean into really enjoying every moment that I can spend climbing. It's such a joy to be back.

## Looking ahead

Having learned that I could take up and enjoy a new sport as an adult, I've decided, why stop with climbing? I'd like next to learn to ride, something I've always liked the idea of but never been in a great position to try. Pre-pandemic, my daughter Lyra enjoyed horse riding lessons and we're wondering about doing some lessons together in the future. I have fond imaginings of trekking through the Welsh valleys on ponies together. If I can just get to the point of getting – and staying – on a horse then I'll take that as a win. Whether or not I go ahead with horse riding, I hope that physical activities that come with a side dose of fun and comradeship will form a big part of my future. I hope I'll be brave enough to continue to try new things, and one thing's for sure, I'll not be hanging up my climbing shoes for a long while yet.

## THINGS YOU COULD TRY

Here are some things you could try if you'd like to apply this lesson to your own life:

1.  **Try something new** – are there any sports or activities that you've always been curious about but haven't been brave enough to try? If so, can you find someone to do a taster with you? It's always less scary than doing it alone.

    *Make a start by* thinking about a sport or activity you'd be interested to try and a friend or colleague you could ask to try it with you:

    . . . . . . . . . . . . . . . . . . . . . . . . . . . . . . . . . . . . . . . . . . . . . . . . . . . . . . . .

    . . . . . . . . . . . . . . . . . . . . . . . . . . . . . . . . . . . . . . . . . . . . . . . . . . . . . . . .

2.  **Smile as you perspire** – if you already have a regular exercise or activity you take part in, just stop and wonder if you're enjoying it as much as you could do. What would make you smile as you perspire? Things that can help include friends to exercise alongside or to have some friendly competition with, or working out to music or with people who make you feel good. Many people (my husband included) are devoted fans of 'Yoga with Adrienne', a YouTuber who creates a safe space for everyone to have fun with yoga in their own time and their own homes. Oh, and her dog regularly features too, which can only be a good thing.

3.  **Try a team sport or join a group** – being part of a team brings a sense of purpose and connection as well as the other advantages of exercise. Find a sport and team that's working at your level and be brave enough to have a go. Something that's important to note here is that many people who did not enjoy team sports at school can go on to really enjoy them as adults, so don't assume it's not for you now just because it didn't float your boat in the past.

# A routine for the day keeps depression (somewhat) at bay

A sustained daily routine can be a game-changer when it comes to being and staying well.

## What I got wrong in the past

In the busyness of day-to-day life, it can be hard to take a step back and see the wood for the trees. Like many young working mums, I found myself constantly running to stand still and went through periods of relative wellness and periods when I was only just about coping (and further periods when I wasn't coping at all).

It felt like a perfectly okay idea to go with the natural ebb and flow of life, and I know it sounds silly, but it had never occurred to me to do anything different. But when I stop and think about it, the periods in my life when I've been most well have been those when I had an enforced routine through work or study, and the times when things fell apart a little were often when that routine was disrupted or removed.

## The lesson and the teacher

This is a lesson I can credit to my daughters, though they were too little to have been consciously teaching us. A particularly interesting and challenging moment in our lives was the point at which Ellie joined our family. She had spent the first six months of her life in foster care and I'd spent the last nine months at home with Lyra since her birth, focusing on her and my PhD while doing a little bit of remote work for our family business (back in the days before remote working was in vogue). As well as two babies, with very different temperaments and life experiences to date, we had to contend with working with the social care system, which included regular 600-mile round trips to meet with Ellie's social care team and birth family.

From that point until when the girls were about three is all a bit of a blur. It was not easy times at all (I hasten to add that it was totally worth it and they are simply brilliant now). One thing I do remember is realizing that we needed to do something to bring the family into some kind of consistent routine. For the first nine months of her life, Lyra had fed and slept on demand whereas Ellie had been sleep trained and had a rigid routine. This is pretty typical for babies in foster care, where the aim is to make it a little easier for their adoptive parents to manage the transition more easily. Ellie came with instructions! She eats at this time, sleeps at this time, gets changed at this time. But of course, we had another, very different baby to contend with too, and somewhere along the line it all got rather muddled.

Both Tom and I got sleep deprived and all thoughts of looking after our own physical and mental wellbeing went out the window as we tried to meet the needs of our girls. After what was probably not too long, but felt like a lifetime, we made a plan. We would create a routine for everyone. We'd have windows for eating and sleeping and also windows for working and resting for me and Tom. Much as we loved each other and the girls, we both also needed time to work and to take a little time out.

While regimented parenting had not been where we'd envisaged ourselves travelling on our parenting journey, it worked wonders for both us and the babies. In particular, eating, sleeping and taking time out at regular times each day made everyone's lives a little easier and meant that Tom and I could guarantee at least a short window each day when both babies were sleeping and we could enjoy each other's company (or collapse exhausted on the sofa).

## What I do now

The power of routine was something the girls taught me during their early years and it's something I've worked hard to maintain ever since. Simple things like eating and sleeping at regular times and building in regular times for work and play make a big difference. Tom and I also build in time to spend together, without the children, and we're both mindful of trying to maintain some sense of routine and rhythm at times when it might naturally dissipate.

I often teach about the power of a daily routine and making small commitments to ourselves about food, exercise, sleep and self-care. It's especially important for the many people I teach who work in the education sector as they have the enforced routine of school broken up with weeks of holidays, when there is no routine at all. While school staff often look forward to these holidays, they also often fall ill physically or find themselves mentally at a low ebb when school stops. There are lots of reasons for this, not least that the routine of school is a strong protective factor during term time, which also brings with it the chance for connection and a sense of purpose.

I'm mindful of my need to break away from my usual routines occasionally to rest and recharge, but I also know that my usual routines need to be replaced with new, temporary ones. In fact, I'm writing this book during a break from my usual routine, hiding away all alone in an Airbnb down in Hastings. While I was craving alone time and needed to reboot my wellbeing, I was very aware that a week of unstructured time was unlikely to be restorative at all. Usually, I'd join an organized group for a week, and have in the past learned to draw or gone canyoning and kayaking in beautiful Slovenia, but the pandemic meant that such excursions were off limits. So, I opted for a solo retreat, with my writing for company. I know when I'll eat and sleep each day, which are my writing hours and at what point I'll walk or knit. It might sound overly controlling and very dull to some of you, but it works for me and is the best way I could think of to ensure that this week is restorative rather than harmful to my mental health – and I hope you're enjoying the fruits of my labour!

## Looking ahead

My girls start secondary school this year, the country is in the process of emerging from a pandemic, we're about to relocate as a family and our business has moved out of its offices to take on an entirely new shape online. It's a time of great change and uncertainty to say the very least, but already we are, as a family, looking ahead and wondering what routines we'd like to adopt in the future.

The girls have asked to put Milkshake Mondays and Fun Fridays in the diary after school once we've moved house and I look forward to welcoming those elements of our new routine. I'll be prioritizing time for climbing and singing, and Tom will make space for squash, and we'll think about how to optimize our life–work balance as our business finds its feet again and we settle in our new home. One routine we'll be certain to bring back is date night – the pandemic put paid to that, but Granny and the girls are looking forward to working out where the best fish and chip shops are near our new home so that they can have their weekly ritual together while Tom and I have a little alone time (which was historically spent climbing and cooking together but who knows what the future may bring). One routine we'll want to keep is our very early morning dog walks and our lunchtime walk and chats; this is a routine Tom and I have fallen into during the pandemic and we love it.

There is a lot that feels uncertain right now, but I'm really looking forward to working out as a family what shape our new routines should take. We'll be making sure that we do the stuff that matters most first and that each of us has the time and space we need each day to do the things that fulfil us, ground us and keep us well.

##  THINGS YOU COULD TRY

Here are some things you could try if you'd like to apply this lesson to your own life:

1. **Consider your current routine** – if you have a routine, consider which bits work well for you and which bits would benefit from a little tweaking. One thing we've found as a family is that making enough time in the mornings, so that we're not all rushing and sniping at each other but rather are having a chat over breakfast and hair plaiting, gets the day off to a far better start. Tom's top tip here is to get everything ready the night before. He's the master of spotting the lost school cardigan or left shoe the night before so it doesn't become a crisis in the morning.

   *Make a start by* listing some tweaks to your current routine which might make it work better for you:

   1. ...................................................................

   2. ...................................................................

   3. ...................................................................

2. **What would add a little joy to your weekly routine?** – maybe you're looking for other things from your life than Milkshake Mondays, but what could you add into your regular routine that would provide little highlights in your week to look forward to?

   *Make a start by* noting down some ideas for regularly scheduled joy:

   1. ...................................................................

   2. ...................................................................

   3. ...................................................................

3.  **Consider what might be worth keeping from your pandemic experience** – the pandemic made us all live very differently and for the most part we might be glad to leave it all behind; but for many of us there might be some new or different ways of doing things that are worth carrying forward. What are yours?

    *Make a start by* noting down the things you'd like to carry forward from the pandemic:

    . . . . . . . . . . . . . . . . . . . . . . . . . . . . . . . . . . . . . . . . . . . . . . . . . . . . . . . . . . .

    . . . . . . . . . . . . . . . . . . . . . . . . . . . . . . . . . . . . . . . . . . . . . . . . . . . . . . . . . . .

    . . . . . . . . . . . . . . . . . . . . . . . . . . . . . . . . . . . . . . . . . . . . . . . . . . . . . . . . . . .

    . . . . . . . . . . . . . . . . . . . . . . . . . . . . . . . . . . . . . . . . . . . . . . . . . . . . . . . . . . .

    . . . . . . . . . . . . . . . . . . . . . . . . . . . . . . . . . . . . . . . . . . . . . . . . . . . . . . . . . . .

    . . . . . . . . . . . . . . . . . . . . . . . . . . . . . . . . . . . . . . . . . . . . . . . . . . . . . . . . . . .

    . . . . . . . . . . . . . . . . . . . . . . . . . . . . . . . . . . . . . . . . . . . . . . . . . . . . . . . . . . .

    . . . . . . . . . . . . . . . . . . . . . . . . . . . . . . . . . . . . . . . . . . . . . . . . . . . . . . . . . . .

    . . . . . . . . . . . . . . . . . . . . . . . . . . . . . . . . . . . . . . . . . . . . . . . . . . . . . . . . . . .

    . . . . . . . . . . . . . . . . . . . . . . . . . . . . . . . . . . . . . . . . . . . . . . . . . . . . . . . . . . .

    . . . . . . . . . . . . . . . . . . . . . . . . . . . . . . . . . . . . . . . . . . . . . . . . . . . . . . . . . . .

    . . . . . . . . . . . . . . . . . . . . . . . . . . . . . . . . . . . . . . . . . . . . . . . . . . . . . . . . . . .

    . . . . . . . . . . . . . . . . . . . . . . . . . . . . . . . . . . . . . . . . . . . . . . . . . . . . . . . . . . .

# Talk to yourself as you'd talk to your dog

We can be so mean to ourselves. What if instead we showed ourselves the love and kindness we show when talking to a favourite pet?

## What I got wrong in the past

Quite how unkind I am when speaking to and about myself has been thrown into sharp relief in recent months as I've done a huge amount of filming and editing of online video-based courses. When I watch back the films of myself where I've made a mistake, I am so evil to myself. Honestly, I find it quite shocking seeing my lip curl and the words of anger spew from my mouth. It's horrible. I wasn't really aware that I do it, though it is something that friends have occasionally remarked on in the past. As you'll have gathered by now, I'm not always thinking the kindest thoughts about myself.

## The lesson and the teacher

Recently, I was editing a video where I had my lovely dog Buddy on my knee. I made a mistake and was busy verbally tearing into myself when Buddy nudged my hand, and my face and my whole posture instantly softened as I cooed over him. I spoke to him only with kindness and reserved the vitriol for myself.

It made me stop and wonder, what if we were as kind to ourselves as we are to our pets? How differently would we feel?

## What I do now

I'm very early on in this journey but it's one that I've shared with the whole family and the girls are especially good at picking me, Tom and Granny up whenever we speak less than kindly about ourselves. Unnecessary apologies are another hot topic around our dinner table too. The first step to change is always acknowledging the scale of the problem and then beginning to try and address it sustainably.

## Looking ahead

I'm still working on it, but now that I've become cognizant of the issue, I'm more frequently catching myself in the process of hating on myself and I literally give myself a good talking to and remind me to be as kind to me as I would be to Buddy. I think it's working and I'm determined to keep trying. Furthermore, I've become bolder about picking up other people who do themselves down. I've found that for many people these patterns are very much entrenched, and many people don't realize they're doing it. It can lead to some really interesting conversations when we open that box and start to explore it.

In particular, this is something I've been exploring with parents and carers. I feel that if we role-model that it's okay to talk unkindly to ourselves about how we look, think or behave then we're telling our children that it's okay to carry that level of self-loathing, when most parents and carers would much prefer that their children were full of self-confidence, care and love.

## ⬇ THINGS YOU COULD TRY

Here are some things you could try if you'd like to apply this lesson to your own life:

1. **Notice negative self-talk and STOP** – this is the first step: just noticing when you're doing it and stopping the thought or

talk in its tracks and then wondering how you'd frame this feedback if it were for a colleague, loved one or pet.

*Make a start by* noting down negative refrains you often repeat about or to yourself:

1. . . . . . . . . . . . . . . . . . . . . . . . . . . . . . . . . . . . . . . . . . . . . . . . . . . . . . . .

2. . . . . . . . . . . . . . . . . . . . . . . . . . . . . . . . . . . . . . . . . . . . . . . . . . . . . . . .

3. . . . . . . . . . . . . . . . . . . . . . . . . . . . . . . . . . . . . . . . . . . . . . . . . . . . . . . .

2. **Challenge self-talk in others** – you may find that they don't even realize they're doing it, but when a friend or colleague starts talking meanly to or about themselves, challenge them about it and ask whether they'd talk to you the same way, and if not, then maybe they should refrain from talking to themselves that way too.

3. **Find moments to talk kindly to yourself** – this is maybe taking the dog thing too far, but one thing we're great at is lavishing our pets with praise when they do the right thing. Maybe as well as doing away with down-talking ourselves, we can start to build in a little bit of positive praise for the stuff we get right (but don't worry, you don't have to eat dog treats).

# Do things just for fun

Doing things for fun, not because we need to or because we're good at them but simply because they make us smile, is a fabulous form of self-care that just keeps on giving.

## What I got wrong in the past

I'm a very productive person. I like to get things done and have spent much of my life and career hyper-focused on goals. This was demonstrated for me when I gave a copy of a book I'd written and just received the proofs of to my therapist because it was dedicated to him, so I thought he might like to see it. He completely changed the topic for the session that day so that we could explore why I seemed in no way proud or moved by the achievement of a book publication but instead was already working towards the next goal.

I have always been driven to achieve things and to do things that can be measured and, like many, many people, I've often shied away from things I'm bad at or that might result in making a fool of myself if I tried and failed. Most notably, though, I found little point in embarking on any activity or endeavour unless I could continually improve and achieve a decent standard in it.

I measured activities by their outcomes rather than by the process. I'm completely reformed in this regard and am now quick to encourage people to pick up long forgotten hobbies or to try their hand at something they've always fancied giving a go.

## The lesson and the teacher

This lesson is one for whom an occupational therapist at the Bethlem Royal Hospital can be largely thanked. Kate, whose ability to listen was matched only by her ability to do beautiful things with clay, ran the pottery studio at the Bethlem and time spent making things with clay was a regular part of the treatment programme for those of us in the eating disorders programme, and some other patients too.

As someone who considered themselves uncreative and bad at art (art GCSE was the only GCSE course to which I was not invited at my school – every teacher wanted me except the art teacher), I was quite daunted by the idea of making things with my hands. I also struggled to see what this had to do with getting better from an eating disorder. However, it did provide me with somewhere calm and quiet and safe to spend my time, which meant that despite my reservations, I went along with it.

When Kate first showed me around the studio, I was puzzled by the shelves and shelves of pottery pieces. Whose were they and why were they here? Kate explained to me that pottery at the Bethlem was much more about the process than the product and that many patients simply never choose to come back and collect their pieces. This baffled me. Why would someone create something and not come back to collect it? 'You'll see,' she said. And I did.

I spent two afternoons a week with Kate up to my elbows in clay and I learned a huge amount. I learned a lot about clay and how to work it; I loved learning different techniques and experimenting with what would work and what wouldn't. I was also interested in the many different glazes and learned to live with the unpredictability of clay as a material. I made huge pieces and tiny pieces. I started again many times, and over time, Kate helped me to see the beauty in the imperfection of pieces I was making and to embrace and embellish those imperfections rather than simply to scrunch the clay up and start again.

The texture of the clay, the calm environment, the gentle music and the delicious earthy smell of the room all made me feel very content and all of my lunchtime anxieties could be worked away through my latest clay creation.

And then it came time for me to leave. I was ready to begin to engage with the world and to leave my intensive day care at the Bethlem behind. You have to be patient with clay; you need to wait days, sometimes weeks, for it to dry before it can be fired and the kiln was only run when there was enough to fill it, so there would often be weeks between a piece being completely made and it being fired and ready to go home. Inevitably, as I'd been pretty prolific, that meant that a lot of my pieces were still waiting to be fired and readied for me at the point at which I was discharged.

Kate made it very clear that I was very welcome to come back to collect my pieces when they were ready in a few weeks' time. But I never returned. The pottery had served its purpose. The power was in the process, not in the product, and so my finished pieces will, I'm sure, have joined the shelves groaning under the weight of patients' past uncollected pieces.

It turns out Kate was right. Of course she was.

## What I do now

Pottery acted like a bit of a gateway into new hobbies for me and into a willingness of doing things simply because I enjoyed doing them. The best example of this is that I took the incredibly brave step of joining my local church choir. One of my favourite things about weddings and funerals has always been the chance to belt out a well-known hymn or two and this is also a fond memory I have of school. I'd not sung (other than in my car or in the shower) for years and years. But I wanted to and Lyra's piano teacher invited her to join the choir he led and I asked if I could come too.

I sing tenor. I find it hard to read complicated choral scores and am forever having to ask questions and get my choir pals to help me, but they happily do. We're a team and I absolutely love the time I spend singing with them. It doesn't matter that

I'm not working towards anything or that I'm not proficiently brilliant. What matters is that, twice a week, St Mary's Church is filled with our voices and my heart is filled with joy.

## Looking ahead

I'm a complete convert to hobbies. One of the things I want to move towards is spending more time doing things that make me smile, regardless of how productive they are (or aren't). I used to have no hobbies, as noted by a psychiatrist who I chose not to remain with, whose letter of diagnosis opened with the words 'Pooky has no hobbies and interests'. The far kinder, better, more wonderful psychiatrist I'm now assigned to is a fellow climber whose first question is always about my climbing. I genuinely think it was a joy for her to see me gain so much from this hobby as when she first met me I was very poorly and too weak to walk.

Since living as a family of five with my mother-in-law as well as Tom and the girls, I've learned to knit; together Granny and I hope to learn to crochet (because she is also a lover of learning to do new things). I'm also learning piano using a brilliant app called *Simply Piano*, which enables me to learn at my own pace and has allowed me to play along to pop songs and classical pieces since I could play my first two notes. I'm also hoping to learn to ride a horse. I'm looking forward to trying out some new things with my girls, both of whom enjoy climbing with me and have expressed an interest in trying out things like paddle boarding and kayaking once we've moved a little closer to some amenable water. I will also continue to build in down-time for myself regularly and use those weeks to climb or walk and sometimes to take up a new hobby. A week I spent pre-pandemic learning to draw while residing in the foothills of Snowdonia was a wonderful way to spend time.

## ⊕ THINGS YOU COULD TRY ▒▒▒▒▒▒▒▒▒▒▒▒

Here are some things you could try if you'd like to apply this lesson to your own life:

1. **Think back to your childhood hobbies** – are there any that you enjoyed that you could take back up?

   *Make a start by* listing past hobbies:

   1. ................................................................

   2. ................................................................

   3. ................................................................

2. **If you had a totally free day with nothing on your to-do list, how would you spend it?** – how can you create a little time for the thing you just named? Planning ahead is often key here, as is perhaps finding a buddy to join you in your activity so you can encourage each other.

   *Make a start by* writing about how you'd most enjoy spending a day:

   ................................................................

   ................................................................

3. **Is there something you've always considered yourself bad at?** – maybe art or music or DIY? If you have a hang up about being unable in a particular domain in life, actually giving it a go can be a great way to slay some long-standing demons. It doesn't mean you have to become a virtuoso at it, but being prepared to try is a great first step. Also, being prepared to have a go at things even if – especially if – we're not proficient at them is brilliant role-modelling for any children in our lives.

   *Make a start by* noting down something that you think you're bad at but which you'd be prepared to try again:

   ................................................................

# Daily don'ts matter as much as daily dos

Commit to the things you promise *not* to do each day and your every day will be a little happier.

## What I got wrong in the past

Even as I was learning to take positive steps towards routine and towards promoting better physical and mental health, there were still many things I was doing every day that were undermining my wellbeing. So as hard as I was working to build it up, I was knocking it right back down again.

## The lesson and the teacher

This lesson is with thanks to Jen and all the young carers that we worked together with during a glorious day of workshops and high ropes. We were working on creating wellbeing action plans that could be used by other young people and one of the elements that we explored together were things to avoid every day.

Working with Jen and this incredible group of young people really opened my eyes to how many dysfunctional habits we each had built into every day. That day, I started to realize the damage that doom-scrolling, constant comparison and negative self-talk were having on my daily life. In addition, I was struggling with self-harm and a toxic friendship. That day, I realized that my path to wellbeing could be helped with routines of doing good things, but it would need to be accompanied by routines of avoiding toxic things.

## What I do now

As well as looking at the positive elements I build into my daily life, I look at the toxic thoughts, behaviours and influences I need to proactively manage. I have an ongoing commitment to myself to try to avoid self-harm every day and I have a very good safety plan in place to help with that. Depending on how things are going, I also sometimes remove myself from particular social media sites, don't allow myself to scroll before bed and think carefully about who I interact with because some people build you up while others are set on dragging you down.

I also go through periods where I cut out alcohol or certain types of books if I'm feeling easily triggered. In addition, noticing and questioning my negative self-talk is an ongoing battle with which I feel as if I'm beginning to make headway.

## Looking ahead

I often talk to people about the benefits of a wellbeing action plan, and in fact many people still use the version that I created with Jen and the young carers that day and which is shared to this day by the Charlie Waller Trust which sends out thousands of copies every year. I try to place as much focus on what we cut out as well as what we add into our daily routines when I'm talking to people. I will continue to try to hold myself to account to the same standards. The next big challenge for me will come with my own daughters who I need to shepherd through the ups and downs of life lived largely online. Many of these lessons were brought forward by lockdown life and the necessity for them to stay connected with their friends somehow, but to date we've still managed to avoid them joining any of the major social networking sites (which is 'so unfair because all our friends have TikTok and Insta').

As ever, I'm sure that helping my girls to navigate their way through adolescence will be a time of great growth and learning for me too. So watch this space.

## ⬇ THINGS YOU COULD TRY ▰▰▰▰▰

Here are some things you could try if you'd like to apply this lesson to your own life:

1.  **Consider what's dragging you down and try to stop it** – think honestly about the way you spend your time each day and be curious about which bits build you up and which bits break you down.

    *Make a start by* listing what is regularly dragging you down:

    1.  . . . . . . . . . . . . . . . . . . . . . . . . . . . . . . . . . . . . . . . . . . . . . . . . . . . . . . . . . . . . . . . .

    2.  . . . . . . . . . . . . . . . . . . . . . . . . . . . . . . . . . . . . . . . . . . . . . . . . . . . . . . . . . . . . . . . .

    3.  . . . . . . . . . . . . . . . . . . . . . . . . . . . . . . . . . . . . . . . . . . . . . . . . . . . . . . . . . . . . . . . .

    4.  . . . . . . . . . . . . . . . . . . . . . . . . . . . . . . . . . . . . . . . . . . . . . . . . . . . . . . . . . . . . . . . .

    5.  . . . . . . . . . . . . . . . . . . . . . . . . . . . . . . . . . . . . . . . . . . . . . . . . . . . . . . . . . . . . . . . .

2.  **Start the discussion with friends and family** – explore with people you trust and care about the kind of things they do each day that drag them down. This can be a really interesting conversation and can often lead to a feeling of 'me too' when we realize that we're struggling with similar things to other people even if we'd not quite noticed before. It's always easier to change habits together.

    *Make a start by* noting down the things that those you trust say are dragging them down:

    1.  . . . . . . . . . . . . . . . . . . . . . . . . . . . . . . . . . . . . . . . . . . . . . . . . . . . . . . . . . . . . . . . .

    2.  . . . . . . . . . . . . . . . . . . . . . . . . . . . . . . . . . . . . . . . . . . . . . . . . . . . . . . . . . . . . . . . .

    3.  . . . . . . . . . . . . . . . . . . . . . . . . . . . . . . . . . . . . . . . . . . . . . . . . . . . . . . . . . . . . . . . .

    4.  . . . . . . . . . . . . . . . . . . . . . . . . . . . . . . . . . . . . . . . . . . . . . . . . . . . . . . . . . . . . . . . .

    5.  . . . . . . . . . . . . . . . . . . . . . . . . . . . . . . . . . . . . . . . . . . . . . . . . . . . . . . . . . . . . . . . .

3.  **Make a start** – just because something isn't good for us, it doesn't mean it's easy to stop. Recognizing that there's something we think we should do less of and taking a small step in the right direction is a great start. Taking that step alongside a friend or loved one will likely increase your chances of success.

    *Make a start by* writing the first step you'll take in a new direction; small sustainable steps work best, for example 'I won't doom scroll after 9pm' or 'I won't automatically say yes to every request' or 'I won't keep sharp objects in my bedroom':

    1.  ................................................................

    2.  ................................................................

    3.  ................................................................

    4.  ................................................................

    5.  ................................................................

Part 4

# LESSONS IN LIFE ONLINE

# Don't compare your bloopers to other people's highlights

When we compare ourselves, warts and all, to other people's airbrushed highlights, it can really knock our self-esteem.

## What I got wrong in the past

My first introduction to not taking everything we see at face value came when working with the Dove Self-Esteem project several years ago, where we used a series of videos to teach children about how those perfect images we see on billboards and in magazines are actually created. A really brilliant video showed the whole process from start to finish, including everything from makeup to clever lighting and photography to image selection and online manipulation of skin and features. The thing that always surprised me the most was that the model's neck was lengthened during the photo-editing process. The model was unrecognizable from start to finish; she probably wished that she looked like the person on the billboards, and yet...it was her.

Back then, the main issue we had to contend with was people comparing themselves to unrealistic images portrayed by the media. Now it's all around us every day, with airbrushing and filters the norm rather than the domain of professional photographers.

Social media is an amazing tool for connection and enabling people to find their tribe, but it also allows us to follow the lives of friends and other people we like or admire and many of us find ourselves constantly comparing ourselves to them.

We don't just compare how we look or what we wear, but how we conduct our daily lives, what our homes look like, how we study or parent, and on it goes. I taught about this, I'd written lesson plans on it and developed training for other trainers, but it's something that I continued to struggle with myself.

I knew that the images were airbrushed and the stories were curated and yet I'd find myself comparing my every day to other people's special day and feeling as if somehow I wasn't quite worthy of my place in society.

## The lesson and the teacher

Ironically, I've learned this lesson from an Instagram influencer. I know, I know. Annie, @theLAminimalist, is a project manager in Los Angeles who posts about 'that not-stuff life' and her journey from huge consumer debt and a very materialistic lifestyle to a minimalist, debt-free life.

Annie's posts are often raw and real and her stories on Instagram are very short but pack a mean punch. I started following her because I'd become interested in consuming less and owning less, but I continued following her for her thoughts on life and how to live well in a broader sense.

Occasionally, Annie will address the fact that other people are trying to be 'like her' and she tells them that they need to just be the best version of themselves that they can be. She never claims to be a perfect minimalist, nor a perfect anything for that matter, but just someone who is trying to live simply, spend more time doing the stuff she loves and build deeper connections with the people in her life.

The lessons I've taken away from Annie have taught me that I'd previously been taking the wrong approach when it came to compare and despair. I'd always thought that what I needed to be doing was simply to switch off those channels, or to try and internalize the idea that the images and stories I was seeing were being shown through a certain filter and should not be compared to my raw shots. What I learned from Annie, and the thing that's made the biggest difference to me, is that it's not about improving the way in which I compare myself, but about becoming more deeply comfortable in myself. When I'm confident that the life I am living, whether or not I choose to share it online, is authentic and brings me joy and challenge and connection and any of the other things I might hope for, then the lives of others will be something I can enjoy and celebrate rather than a stick with which to beat myself.

## What I do now

I'm not at that point of perfect inner contentment and contemplation yet and I currently still find it very helpful to limit my access to social media sites such as Facebook and Instagram. In particular, these two sites tend to make me feel as if I'm a less good parent than I should be and I find that the heavy use of images and filters can warp my sense of reality and create unrealistic ideals that I still find myself attempting to aspire to.

So I limit my access to social media. But I'm doing some deeper work too. The pandemic has been a great time of reflection for me and my family and we're making some pretty fundamental changes to our day-to-day life. Are they changes that would look eye-catching on social media? Probably not. But are they changes that will lead to a deeper sense of fulfilment and more joy every day? I very much hope so.

## Looking ahead

I'll continue trying to work towards a simpler, more fulfilling way of life for myself and my family which I believe will be the very best protection from compare and despair and will mean we're happy and healthy to boot. I'm also beginning to think about my own use of social media. I've become aware recently that other people sometimes compare their life to mine in just the way I've been guilty of comparing my life to others'. I find myself wondering if there is a more authentic way to use sites like Instagram. I've already made this effort on Twitter and am careful to be open and honest about the harder days as well as the better ones. But other social networks are more difficult, especially when they're image based, because just how often do we take a photograph of the mundanity of everyday life or challenge that we're struggling with? And how compelled do we feel to tell those stories?

This is something I need to do more thinking on, and as my girls reach an age where they will soon begin to curate their lives online, I look forward to exploring this with them and their friends.

## ⬇ THINGS YOU COULD TRY

Here are some things you could try if you'd like to apply this lesson to your own life:

1. **Look at your own social media stream** – notice what you've chosen to share and imagine how someone who didn't know you would interpret your life. Would it give them a realistic understanding of who you are and how your life is? If not, is that a problem? Maybe not, but just hold that thought when lusting after others' lives.

   *Make a start by* noting down what you notice about your social media streams:

   . . . . . . . . . . . . . . . . . . . . . . . . . . . . . . . . . . . . . . . . . . . . . . . . . . . . . . . .

   . . . . . . . . . . . . . . . . . . . . . . . . . . . . . . . . . . . . . . . . . . . . . . . . . . . . . . . .

   . . . . . . . . . . . . . . . . . . . . . . . . . . . . . . . . . . . . . . . . . . . . . . . . . . . . . . . .

2. **Wonder 'Why are they telling this story?'** – when viewing the stories that other people share, if they leave you with a feeling of envy or emptiness or discontent, just take a moment to wonder what the story is that this person is trying to tell

and why. Often, people work very hard to portray the life they'd like to live rather than the one they are actually living.

3. **Limit the time you spend comparing and despairing** – be aware of the time you spend on social media sites and consider how long and when you should be spending that time. For example, it can be helpful to avoid this behaviour just before bed as it can leave you with feelings of inadequacy swirling round and round in your head as you try to sleep.

*Make a start by* listing any 'rules' you'd like to try and make around your social media usage:

1. .........................................................

2. .........................................................

3. .........................................................

# If you wouldn't share it with your gran, don't share it

You're going to tea with your gran; if you wouldn't wear a t-shirt emblazoned with the words or images you're thinking of sharing then you shouldn't share them.

### What I got wrong in the past

It can be easy to forget that when we share things online they are there for ever (often even if we delete them) and we never know quite who will read them or how they'll be interpreted.

I was lucky enough to have made it to adulthood before the emergence of social media or I'm sure I'd have some far worse stories to tell here. Fortunately, this is a secondhand mistake borrowed from a student whose class I worked with and who had made the mistake of sharing intimate photos of his girlfriend in a private group online. You can guess the rest; he lost the girlfriend, lost the respect of a lot of people around him, got into a lot of trouble and spent months struggling with the subsequent impact on his mental health.

### The lesson and the teacher

This time, the teacher is me. I've long used 'Would you wear it to tea with your gran?' as the yardstick for what to share and what not to online. In workshops with young people, it seemed to help them to really 'get it' because while their ideas about what was and wasn't acceptable in terms of sharing via their phones, laptops or tablets might have been a little confused, they tended to have a very clear idea of what their gran would approve of. Grans are great like that.

We won't get it right one hundred per cent of the time, but it's important that we think before we share because our digital lives have the potential to hurt, embarrass or otherwise upset others as well as ourselves. Occasionally an impulse or moment of poor judgement years ago can come back to haunt us as every word and image we share is like a digital tattoo that could be mined by someone so minded in the future.

## What I do now

That all sounds very gloomy. It's not meant to! The 'Gran Test' is simply designed as a quick method for checking before we share. The answer is usually pretty unequivocal (unless you have/had a very unconventional gran, in which case maybe borrow someone else's for this exercise).

I still use this question and others like it many times a day. For email as well as for use of social media and messaging apps. I also ask myself whether I'd be happy for the person I'm talking about to read what I'm writing, and finally, I've found the three gates of speech which my daughters were taught at school to be helpful:

1. Is it true?
2. Is it necessary?
3. Is it kind?

Our words online and offline should pass successfully through these three gates before they are spoken or shared.

## Looking ahead

As well as continuing to try to share appropriately online, another step I'm keen to take is to tackle head on the moments when I get it wrong. These moments are usually because my meaning has landed differently from what was intended. It is very easy for meaning to get lost online. I think it's important that I own those moments and try to learn from them so that I can try to avoid them happening again. This doesn't happen often, I'm pretty boring online as I hate to court controversy. However, I do have a tendency to hide from awkwardness, but I think I could learn and grow a little by opening up a dialogue with those with whom my words or ideas have landed less well.

## ⬇ THINGS YOU COULD TRY

Here are some things you could try if you'd like to apply this lesson to your own life:

1. **Use the 'Gran Test'** – if unsure whether to share something online, consider how you'd feel taking tea with your gran wearing a t-shirt showing those words or images.

2. **Use the three gates** – only share your words if they can pass through the three gates. Is it true? Is it necessary? Is it kind?

3. **Be curious when things go wrong** – if your words land differently from how you intended them to, wonder why and try to course correct.

# Don't feed the trolls

While our first instinct is always to defend ourselves and fight back, I've found silence to be the most effective tool when it comes to managing trolls online.

## What I got wrong in the past

If someone is unkind, critical or just downright rude to or about us, it's human nature to want to stick up for ourselves and this used to be my response too. I didn't come across this situation much until I started working in social media and then, when I was the voice of a more corporate account with a far wider reach, I suddenly found that every now and then I'd run into keyboard warriors who would either belittle me, my employers or the people who wrote for us.

Naturally, I tried to respond to these incoming messages, to try to change points of view or share wider context. These words in turn would often be skewed or quoted out of context. It was a bit of a lose-lose situation.

## The lesson and the teacher

This was a lesson that came via a teacher who followed both my personal accounts and the ones I was running for my employer. Krishnan shared some advice that really helped me. He was looking from the outside in and could see things far more clearly than I could while deeply entrenched in my interactions, good and bad, every day. He pointed out to me a couple of key things:

first, that bullies are always looking to provoke a reaction, and second, that I had a far larger network than the bullies.

With this in mind, he suggested that instead of responding and adding fuel to the fire, I simply allowed the comments to quietly die. Like many bullies, these online trolls would soon get bored if they didn't get the reaction they were looking for. What's more, by not responding, I'd be ensuring that their unkindness was seen by only a few (their network) rather than by many (my network).

It was difficult advice to follow because it went against every natural instinct I had, but it worked an absolute treat and 'do not feed the trolls' is an adage I've lived by for many years now.

## What I do now

I continue not to feed the trolls and have learned to make liberal use of block and mute functions. If people are spoiling for a fight, they've picked the wrong person. Again and again, I've been amazed how people just slink away if you don't give them the satisfaction of a reaction.

One thing I did get wrong once was to share a comment that someone had made to me on LinkedIn that had left me reeling and baffled. I tweeted a screenshot not because I wanted anyone to respond to the comment but because I wanted to check whether anyone could elaborate on this point of view, or help me understand whether I should be doing things differently or better.

Within minutes, my lovely network were piling in on this man on LinkedIn. In their kind defence of me, they were pretty unkind to him. As soon as I realized what was happening, I deleted the tweet and published another asking people not to comment on LinkedIn. The context entirely escapes me now, but I do remember feeling guilty for how this onslaught must have made the commentor feel. I've never since shared these kinds of comments because trolls are people too and I often find myself wondering about how someone must be feeling in order to make such comments in the first place.

## Looking ahead

There is definitely no troll-feeding in my future. The one thing that is changing is the way I'd like to use my presence online. I've lived a pretty uncontroversial life online for many years because I find conflict difficult and have always been wary about expressing an opinion on topics where I know there are strong and polarized feelings. However, there are some big topics that I do have strong opinions on, and opinions that are backed by scientific evidence and where the contrary opinion has the real potential to do harm to children and young people. I no longer feel that in order to have a calm and quiet life I can keep quiet. I need to be braver in using my voice, but in doing so, I need to think really carefully about how to manage the feedback I get because no matter how good I get at ignoring malicious, unsubstantiated words, it's not easy and may feel harder if there is more of it to contend with.

## ⊕ THINGS YOU COULD TRY

Here are some things you could try if you'd like to apply this lesson to your own life:

1. **Simply don't respond** – if someone is spoiling for a fight, just ignore them.

2. **If you must respond, write it, save it, then send it** – never respond in the heat of the moment. Either wait for some time to elapse and write your response when you are feeling calmer, or write your response and save it in draft and reread and edit it before sending it. Slowing down interactions like this will take some of the heat from the flames, compared to a quick-fire back and forth, and will give you time to ensure

that your response is considered and reasonable and not open to misinterpretation.

3. **Work out your anger by writing and ripping** – it can be hard not to respond to really horrible things said to us even if we know that it's the best course of action. Often, we have so much anger and rage bubbling up inside us that it needs an outlet. My favourite thing to do in this situation is to write a response, with good old-fashioned pen and paper, getting out everything I need to say. And then I tear it into tiny, tiny, tiny shreds before continuing with my day. It works wonders.

# Delete the bad comments, file the good ones

Deleting negative and unkind comments while making efforts to save positive feedback can have a big impact on our experience online.

## What I got wrong in the past

Historically, I was always pretty good at tuning in to negative feedback, no matter what form it took. I realized the extent of this maladaptive behaviour when I presented a session at a youth mental health conference for a major charity a few years ago. Feedback scores were collated from the 600 attendees and shared with all speakers. In my first analysis of this feedback, all I could see was one glaring negative piece of feedback. Someone had marked my session as less than good and I couldn't get it out of my head. I felt as if I'd totally failed. It was only when the people who'd commissioned me to run the session called me to ask me to work for them again because I'd had the best set of feedback they'd ever seen that I looked at that feedback through a different lens.

I had zoned straight in on the one negative piece of feedback and completely disregarded the 599 people who'd rated my talk as very good or outstanding. Why did this one piece of negative feedback have such power over me? Well, it's quite a common thing and is part of a negative automatic thought process that happens for a lot of people who struggle with issues like depression, anxiety or low self-esteem. It's called 'mental filtering' and results in us filtering out certain types of evidence, in this case positive feedback, and focusing in on other types of evidence, in this case negative feedback.

It happens because as humans we are continuously on the lookout for evidence that backs up our existing point of view. That day, as someone who had a very negative view of myself and my abilities, I'd been focusing on evidence that backed up that point of view and I'd discarded evidence that disputed it.

Any reasonable person can see that 599 out of 600 is a pretty decent score and I was able to concede in the end that I'd done an objectively good job. Realizing quite how wonky my thought process was with this very clear example caused me to mentally stop and start to wonder how many other areas of my life this was impacting on.

## The lesson and the teacher

This is one of those lessons where my thinking really consolidated when I became the teacher for my daughters. Lyra and Ellie enjoy making occasional YouTube videos together and sharing them online. They've made videos about all sorts of things and, on the whole, they get kind and positive feedback from people. Just occasionally, someone will say something mean; at first this would really upset them, and I'd see echoes of my former self zoning in on the negative and ignoring the positive.

The thing with online comments and YouTube is that your videos get viewed by far more people than those who choose to interact with them, and once your video is released into the wild then you have no control over who will see it or what they'll say. This can be exciting when you see the views rack up and you're receiving likes and the occasional positive comment, but it's a hard bump down to earth when someone writes something mean.

As my own channels have grown and I receive more and more comments (both positive and negative) on my back catalogue of content as well as the new stuff, I've developed a strict process for managing incoming comments. I use this elsewhere online and in life, but most judiciously on YouTube.

I briefly read comments and I categorize them in my head as Good, Bad or Constructive. The bad comments – those that are wholly negative, mean or unsubstantiated, and are simply someone being nasty because for some reason people just do that sometimes – I delete right away, without a second thought.

The deleting is important – this is my channel and I get to choose what's shared there. I've also found that once one person is unkind, others can tend to pile in having been given permission for their unkindness by that first comment. It's a bit like the way bullies might gang up on a victim. So I check regularly, and simply delete any nastiness.

Some negative comments are actually important to me though, and these are the constructive comments. Sometimes the negative feedback has some basis that could be helpful to me; comments on my earlier videos from non-English speakers that I speak too fast have helped me (I think) over the years to slow down and speak in a more measured and clear way. I will act on these comments, and if I'm unsure if the comment is a fair reflection, I'll ask for further feedback from people I trust. It can be hard to invite constructive criticism, but it really is a great way to learn.

Finally, the good comments. Most of them I do nothing with, but occasionally there will be one that is just *so good*, one that reminds me why I do what I do, and that leaves me beaming from head to toe. Comments that show me I've made a difference to someone, and that my words have had an impact, I keep. I have a file which I can access from my computer and phone called 'Nice Things People Have Said'. The really good stuff goes in here and I keep it. And occasionally, on the really bad days or if I've just read a really vicious, negative comment, I refer back to this file.

I also photograph thank you cards and screenshot emails and keep them in this file. It all goes in there. This 'evidence bank' was originally suggested by my therapist Mat, who'd noted that I seem to get a lot of incredible feedback but do not give it the attention it deserves.

Explaining and role-modelling this process to my girls really helped to clarify my thinking on it, and seeing things through the lens of a mum can often put things in sharper relief for me too. I sometimes wonder on my own channels if it's not morally wrong to delete repugnant comments, but I do so without thinking on their channels. Of course those comments should be deleted; I'd burn them if I could – how dare people.

YouTube has since updated the way things work so that children's videos no longer get comments at all, but I hope that these early discussions about deleting the bad and filing the good will stand my girls in good stead.

## What I do now

As well as continuing to delete the bad and filing the good, I increasingly encourage others to do the same. This can be especially helpful for people who struggle with feelings of imposter syndrome. Having a file of nice things that people have said can be super helpful, and evidence from people you respect and trust that they think you're doing a good job is hard to dispute, no matter how down on yourself you might be feeling.

## Looking ahead

One thing I'd like to do is to try and redress the balance of good and bad comments online. We are often far quicker to criticize than to compliment. We'll often view without comment something that we find to be helpful while we might take the time to complain if something is not of a standard we'd hoped for. I'll be actively noticing how many comments I make of each type online, trying to be constructive in any criticism I may levy and making a little more effort to share the positives.

Most of all, I always try to remember that there is a human behind the massive YouTube channel, Instagram account or Twitter network. I wonder if would I say this to a person face-to-face; if I would then I make my comment, if I'm not sure, I don't.

**THINGS YOU COULD TRY**

Here are some things you could try if you'd like to apply this lesson to your own life:

1. **Delete, block and mute if necessary** – take control of the messages you see by deleting what is unkind and unhelpful or muting or blocking people who are unkind. You're in charge here.

2. **Consider what you'd advise a friend to do** – if you find it hard to block, delete or mute a comment, imagine you were advising a friend in the same situation. What would you tell them to do about this comment? Try to extend the same kindness to yourself.

3. **Create a 'Nice Things People Have Said' file** – keep positive feedback here and refer back to it on more difficult days.

# Actively curate your social media feeds

Take control of what and who is in your social media feeds to make this a safe and positive space rather than one that drags you down.

## What I got wrong in the past

I used to let my social media feeds bring my mood down. I followed lots of sources of news (have you ever noticed how more bad news gets shared than good news?) and people who were doing life so much better than I could hope to, which led to constant comparisons and despair.

## The lesson and the teacher

My friend Natasha has been my best teacher here. In particular, when we were both speaking at a conference for teens, hearing her talking about taking an active approach to curating your social media feeds really struck home with me.

She talked cogently about how we own our social media feeds, we get to choose who we follow and unfollow and, especially if we spend a lot of time online, the choices that we make about who and what make up our feed will have a big impact on how we feel.

Until that point, my timelines had grown organically through meeting people or reciprocal following. I often added news sources or people who interested me or whose pictures I found visually appealing to my feed. I was following a lot of people but not all of them added to a sense of wellbeing. Lots of them were just noise, people I didn't really know or whose lives were so removed from mine that their posts felt inconsequential to me, or brands or causes that I'd once been interested in but had never made the active decision to unfollow as life moved on.

Natasha's approach was very different. She suggested that we could turn our social media feeds into inspirational channels that spurred us into action, that helped us to live a contented life or simply made us smile. The first step is to understand what you'd like to get from your life online – why you engage with it – and then to carefully curate who you follow, and who you don't, to help you achieve that goal.

## What I do now

It sounds simple and in essence it is. The first big clear out is very satisfying, saying goodbye to all those accounts that have been quietly eroding your mood or self-esteem for the longest time. Finding brilliant accounts to follow can also be quite rewarding. Reaching out to your network or searching online for people or hashtags to follow that sit well with your ideologies can be a great rabbit hole to leap into for an hour or two.

The hard bit comes with keeping it up. Every few months, I proactively look at who I'm following and think carefully about which channels I'm using for what and I go through the whole process again of following, unfollowing and redefining the meaning of my online life. It's forever changing of course, and there is always room for new positive influences and people whose messages bring a little joy, or which stretch and challenge my way of thinking.

## Looking ahead

I've got a lot more work to do here but I'm happier online than I have been in the past. I try to be intentional and deliberate in the channels I use and the people, brands and causes I interact with. I love it when I can use my platform to amplify the voices and ideas of others and I've tried to move away from feeling guilty for spending time on social media.

When that time is intentional and it builds me rather than breaks me, in the right doses it can be a really positive use of time. It does require continuous reflection and course correction though.

## ⊕ THINGS YOU COULD TRY ▨▨▨▨▨▨

Here are some things you could try if you'd like to apply this lesson to your own life:

1.  **Decide what you'd like from your life online** – social media can often just be a way to pass time. What if you were more deliberate and decided that this is a space you want to use to make you laugh, or to learn, or to build connections with people with similar outlooks to yourself?

    *Make a start by* listing what you'd like from your life online:

    1.  .........................................................

    2.  .........................................................

    3.  .........................................................

2.  **Carry out a cull** – it sounds heartless but these are your time-lines and you have the right to own them. Unfollow, delete, mute or otherwise remove people, brands and causes which are no longer of interest to you or which drag you down. On some sites, you can also choose not to see certain adverts; this can be really worth doing. In particular, as someone with a history of anorexia, I always try to opt out of the endless adverts about weight loss that I'm served with.

3.  **Find accounts to follow that make your heart sing** – ask for recommendations or search online for lists of people, brands and hashtags that align with the life you'd like to have online. Adding positive influences and influencers to your timeline as

well as removing the negative ones can make social media a far more positive space in which to hang out.

*Make a start by* writing a list of the kinds of people, brands or hashtags you'd like to interact with more:

1. ...................................................................

2. ...................................................................

3. ...................................................................

4. ...................................................................

5. ...................................................................

# Don't touch your phone before breakfast

When our first action of the day is to check our emails and our social media and news feeds, we allow our whole day to be dictated by external influences.

### What I got wrong in the past

What is the first thing you do when you wake up? Reach for your phone and check your emails, the news and your social media feeds? Me too, or at least it's what I used to do. For years and years and years. I'm not sure why this habit developed for me, but it's a pretty common one. It's not a great way to start your day, though, when you really stop and think about it. The news is almost universally negative; your emails are full of other people's to-dos which you end up taking on, and social media is an unpredictable beast, certainly not a space you can rely on as a positive start to the day.

### The lesson and the teacher

This lesson came from Dimpna, who told me that she never touched her phone until after breakfast. She said that by the time she'd got up and dressed, had breakfast and settled into the day, she was ready to engage with the outside world. Before that point, she did not want the world outside her home to dictate how she thought or felt.

This resonated with me, first because I love a binary rule – they're so easy to follow – and second because, on reflection, I realized that those first few minutes in the day are really crucial and how I chose to spend them could dictate how I thought, felt and acted much of the rest of the morning, if not the whole day.

I didn't start right away, but rather observed myself for a few days to see if this urge to check in on the outside world really was impacting on my mornings. I'm a scientist at heart and I needed a baseline to work from. I noticed that my mood was hugely affected by how my phone told me to feel. My children would have a far kinder, more patient and jolly mum on the days when the first things I read or saw were positive, but most days I'd notice that I was uptight, rushing them and being snappy with them, and this was often not about them but about an email that was niggling with me or something in the news that had darkened my mood.

I decided to give Dimpna's idea a try and I banned myself from interacting with my phone at all until at least after I'd eaten breakfast. I found that the world did not stop turning on its axis if I didn't check in with Twitter first thing, and those emails really could wait. I also found that I was able to be a far nicer mum to my girls as we readied for the day ahead when my mood hadn't been dampened and I wasn't distracted with my phone in my hand.

## What I do now

Currently I leave my phone by my bed (where it resides only because I listen to audio books as I fall asleep) and I leave it on 'do not disturb' while my husband and I get up for our early morning dog walk. I then return home and get the children up and breakfasted. I try not to touch my phone during this time. As we're leaving the house, I pick my phone up as it provides our music for the commute into school and it's only then that I turn 'do not disturb' off, but I'm driving so I don't interact with my phone. So it's usually not until I get home at about 9am that I interact with the online world for the first time. This is hours later than I used to, and the first chance I have to properly digest emails and messages.

I don't manage it every day, but I have found that having this as my standard way of doing things has made a really big difference.

## Looking ahead

One thing I've particularly noticed is that half reading emails on my phone at any time of day when I'm not in a position to fully read and respond can cause a spike in anxiety. I misread and misinterpret things and often they circle in my head. So many times, I've found that when I actually sit down at my desk and read an email properly, everything is better than I thought and I've spent my time needlessly worrying.

This has made me wonder about completely removing email from my phone. It feels like a big step and one I'm not quite ready for yet, but I can't help but feel that only reading emails and other messages when I'm in a position to properly digest and action might prove beneficial.

## ⊕ THINGS YOU COULD TRY

Here are some things you could try if you'd like to apply this lesson to your own life:

1.  **Notice how your early online interactions affect your mood** – at first, simply be curious. If you check your phone first thing, does it impact on how you feel, think or behave?

    *Make a start by* noting down how you feel after you check your phone first thing each day for a week:

    Day 1. . . . . . . . . . . . . . . . . . . . . . . . . . . . . . . . . . . . . . . . . . . . . . . . . . . . . . . .

    Day 2. . . . . . . . . . . . . . . . . . . . . . . . . . . . . . . . . . . . . . . . . . . . . . . . . . . . . . . .

    Day 3. . . . . . . . . . . . . . . . . . . . . . . . . . . . . . . . . . . . . . . . . . . . . . . . . . . . . . . .

    Day 4. . . . . . . . . . . . . . . . . . . . . . . . . . . . . . . . . . . . . . . . . . . . . . . . . . . . . . . .

**Day 5.** . . . . . . . . . . . . . . . . . . . . . . . . . . . . . . . . . . . . . . . . . . . . . . . . . . . . . . . .

**Day 6.** . . . . . . . . . . . . . . . . . . . . . . . . . . . . . . . . . . . . . . . . . . . . . . . . . . . . . . . .

**Day 7.** . . . . . . . . . . . . . . . . . . . . . . . . . . . . . . . . . . . . . . . . . . . . . . . . . . . . . . . .

2. **Do a trial** – set yourself a challenge of three days or a week without checking your phone before breakfast. Again, be curious about how you feel, think and behave. Is it different?

   *Make a start by* writing down what you'd like to try and do and for how long:

   . . . . . . . . . . . . . . . . . . . . . . . . . . . . . . . . . . . . . . . . . . . . . . . . . . . . . . . .

   . . . . . . . . . . . . . . . . . . . . . . . . . . . . . . . . . . . . . . . . . . . . . . . . . . . . . . . .

   . . . . . . . . . . . . . . . . . . . . . . . . . . . . . . . . . . . . . . . . . . . . . . . . . . . . . . . .

   . . . . . . . . . . . . . . . . . . . . . . . . . . . . . . . . . . . . . . . . . . . . . . . . . . . . . . . .

   . . . . . . . . . . . . . . . . . . . . . . . . . . . . . . . . . . . . . . . . . . . . . . . . . . . . . . . .

   . . . . . . . . . . . . . . . . . . . . . . . . . . . . . . . . . . . . . . . . . . . . . . . . . . . . . . . .

3. **Create a rule and try to stick to it** – if, like me, you find it helps your mood not to check your phone before breakfast, try to create a rule that you feel you can stick to. Maybe your phone stays on 'do not disturb' and out of reach until 8am, for example. It's often easier to adhere to a black and white rule; you can always change the rule and adapt it a little if it's not quite working for you.

   *Make a start by* writing the rules you'd like to try and live by once you've had a chance to experiment a little to see what makes a difference:

   1. . . . . . . . . . . . . . . . . . . . . . . . . . . . . . . . . . . . . . . . . . . . . . . . . . . .

   2. . . . . . . . . . . . . . . . . . . . . . . . . . . . . . . . . . . . . . . . . . . . . . . . . . . .

   3. . . . . . . . . . . . . . . . . . . . . . . . . . . . . . . . . . . . . . . . . . . . . . . . . . . .

# Look for good things and they'll become more abundant

> When you get in the habit of sharing positive things online, you'll find that people reciprocate with positivity, which can make your online space a far happier one.

### What I got wrong in the past

As I've mentioned before, I didn't used to have a particular drive or purpose to my online interactions. This wasn't necessarily a terrible thing, as I've learned a lot and made some great friends over the years from sporadic and sometimes random communications online. But I have found that being more focused, and in particular ending each day with positives, has had a really lovely impact on my interactions both online and offline.

### The lesson and the teacher

A few years ago, I was lucky enough to be invited to attend a talk by Marty Seligman who'd been flown in by a big bank in Canary Wharf I'd done a little training for. Marty Seligman is considered the godfather of positive psychology and that day he shared the results of an experiment which has changed the course of my every day ever since.

The experiment was about gratitude journalling and the research showed that, in a large sample, people who wrote about three things they were grateful for at the end of each day found that over time their wellbeing scores increased. This increase was maintained for several weeks after the experiment ended. The control group did non-directive journalling and this did not have the same impact on mood.

In the original experiment, people had privately journalled about three things they were grateful for in a traditional paper journal. They'd been encouraged to include as much detail as they could. I was impressed with the results and it got me wondering whether I could build a similar daily habit. I've never managed to stick with writing a journal so I was worried I wouldn't keep it up. I decided instead to turn to Twitter, where I've been sharing #3GoodThings almost every day ever since.

The very nature of Twitter means that these are short and sweet reflections on my day. They are often accompanied by pictures, which I think is a real benefit over traditional journalling. The other benefit of using Twitter is that other people join in too. Over the years, more and more people have joined me in sharing their three good things each day; I actively invite this by always including 'Yours?' at the end of my tweet after I've written my daily list of three.

## What I do now

I don't remember when I started sharing #3GoodThings but I've done it almost daily for years now. As well as providing me with a lovely way to look back on positive memories and to find a little joy in each day and share in other people's joy too, it's also helped me on more difficult days. Some days it's hard to find three good things because everything feels dark and difficult. These are the days that it matters more than ever for me to find little moments of joy in the day. I'll sometimes preface these tweets with 'tough one today' or similar, or on an especially hard day I'll sometimes ask my followers to go first as I'm struggling. Reading other people's positives often helps to lift me and helps me succeed in seeking out my own positives. I try to live by the adage that not every day is a good day, but there is good in every day.

This daily habit has, I think, fundamentally helped me to think differently. I often find myself noticing small good things throughout the day and might take a moment longer to appreciate a beautiful sight, sound or smell, or to capture a happy or funny moment in a photograph I can include in my tweets. It also means that I often look for the positives in a situation I'd have found to be negative in the past. My favourite example is that I now love it when I'm faced with heavy traffic as I know that I'll have more undisturbed time to listen to my audio book. A luxury borne out of a situation that used to be simply stressful.

An interesting outcome from my daily habit of sharing #3GoodThings is the reception I get offline now. #3GoodThings is the thing I most consistently share online and for some reason seems to get bounced to the top of people's timelines. Presumably, Twitter's algorithms note the amount of interaction on these tweets. This means that for many people, on meeting me for the first time, the thing they most associate with me is this daily habit. It often means that interactions with new people start on a very positive note, which is a lovely way to commence.

When I heard Marty Seligman speak and started looking for good things every day, I decided to give it a go because I was not in a good way. I was having some very dark days and struggling a lot with depression, suicidal ideation and self-harm. I wanted things to feel different but was struggling to make that change happen. This felt like a small thing that was achievable and that the evidence suggested might be worth a go. It was one of many things which helped me work towards better wellbeing, but it's certainly been significant and many people I've worked with or taught over the years have adopted it as a strategy in their personal or working lives to great effect too.

## Looking ahead

I will continue to share #3GoodThings every day and encourage others to do the same; if you haven't already, perhaps you'd like to join us on Twitter? We're a very friendly bunch.

While, as I've mentioned earlier in this book, I try to keep my interactions online authentic and honest, I've found great benefit in making the effort to look for positives no matter how small. Having regular interactions with other people about the positives of either my day or theirs is a great way to ensure that my timeline is sprinkled with smiles, which is just how I like it.

 ## THINGS YOU COULD TRY

Here are some things you could try if you'd like to apply this lesson to your own life:

1. **Write down three good things every day** – either join us online or go old style with a traditional journal.

   *Make a start by* listing today's three good things:

   1. ....................................................................

   2. ....................................................................

   3. ....................................................................

2. **Notice little things that make you happy throughout the day** – even if you don't choose to write them down or share them, just making an effort to notice the good things can make them loom larger in your life.

3. **Look for the good side in things** – when things don't go to plan, challenge yourself to find an unexpected upside to the situation.

   *Make a start by* thinking about a recent situation that was negative and hunting for the positive flipside:

   ....................................................................

   ....................................................................

   ....................................................................

# Part 5

# LESSONS IN DEATH AND DYING

# Don't leave it too late to plan for death

While it can feel very hard to have conversations about death and dying, these conversations can provide us with the knowledge we need to carry out a loved one's wishes.

## What I got wrong in the past

I used to hide my head in the sand when it came to death and dying. When we love someone, the thought of them dying can be too hard to bear and sometimes the conversations that we most need to have are the last ones we end up having.

In particular, I almost got this very wrong with my grandfather, whom I have doted on ever since I can remember and who walked me down the aisle when I married Tom. After the loss of my grandmother, we spent a lot of time in each other's company in the decade before his eventual death. I was his legal next of kin and it was to me that heads would eventually turn when there were difficult decisions to be made.

But I lived in oblivion, and any time he tried to turn the conversation towards death and dying, I changed the topic. I was unable to talk about it and jokily responded that he wasn't allowed to die, that he was immortal and would be here forever.

## The lesson and the teacher

Of course, my grandfather didn't live forever, and after a little time living with my family, he eventually moved into the most wonderful care home which was near to our home and allowed me to step back from being his carer and return to being his granddaughter. At the point that he moved into the home, I assumed we had many years of crosswords and tea drinking ahead of us, and so when Emmanuel, one of the care workers, arranged a meeting to discuss my grandfather's wishes about death and dying, I was floored.

I felt quite affronted as I 'knew' that my grandfather had years and years ahead of him and to have these discussions about his death felt insensitive and strangely like tempting fate. Emmanuel assured me that it was better to have these conversations in good time, that they in no way suggested that death was imminent but meant that we'd have a written record of my grandfather's wishes that we could refer back to in the future. This record could, he assured me, be changed if my grandfather's wishes changed over time.

It should be noted that Grandpa was completely at ease talking about death and dying. He seemed at peace with the idea that he might not be around a lot longer; it was me who was the problem. Emmanuel talked us through all the questions and the three of us had one of the most difficult conversations of my life because it forced me to face Grandpa's mortality. But, within an hour, I knew exactly what Grandpa would want to happen in the case of a medical emergency, I knew what kind of funeral he wanted and I understood his expectations of me as an executor. I knew exactly what he wanted me to do.

Grandpa didn't live for many more months after that conversation, and throughout the process of illness, death, dying and the aftermath, I was able to feel that every decision that I made on his behalf I was making with his blessing. There were some decisions that I'd have made very differently had we not had that conversation, so I'll always be grateful to Emmanuel, whose quiet certainty and guidance helped me to be the best granddaughter I could be.

## What I do now

I am no longer afraid of conversations about death and dying. I think it's really important to make our wishes known and to be able to have open and honest conversations long ahead of time. Things change and our wishes may change with them, so it's important to revisit the conversation every now and then. Conversations about death and dying are not something we've shied away from as a family of five. One of the jobs my mother-in-law is currently doing is putting all her jewellery into boxes and explaining to Lyra what each piece is, where it came from and who she'd like to leave it to. She's doing this job with Lyra as during a recent clearing out session we stumbled on all the jewellery boxes and she told me that when she died I'd need to put the jewellery back in the right boxes and dish it out. I told her, honestly, that in the event of her death I'd have other things on my mind than marrying up the jewellery with the boxes and that I'd be more likely to throw the boxes away unless they were sorted out in the meantime.

So she's sorting them out, and the job will fall to Lyra, who is far more interested in such things (my strengths lie elsewhere). For the two of them, this sorting process has been a lovely source of conversation and Lyra has learned a lot about her predecessors from whom much of the jewellery came. It sounds like a little thing, but if we'd not been able to have an open conversation about it, no one would have known where to start. There will, I'm sure, be lots of little things like this we'll learn over the coming years, and we no longer shy away from conversations about death just because it's not imminent.

Other people's funerals are always a good moment to reflect on our own, and ever since they were tiny, I've taken the girls to funerals of loved ones and allowed them to ask as many questions as they need to. A priest, who I thought was going to tell me off, once praised this behaviour when he came to talk to me and three-year-old Lyra, who was peering down into her Great Grandpa Geoff's grave and wondering if it would be okay to get in and tickle his feet.

Talking about it more doesn't make death or dying easy, but one day in the far-off future when it's the turn of me or my husband to go, this rich tapestry of conversations throughout a lifetime will, I hope, mean our girls feel as confident enacting our wishes as I felt enacting my grandfather's.

### Looking ahead

We'll keep talking about dying and death and ensuring that it's not a taboo topic in our household. It's as natural a part of life as birth, so we shouldn't shy away from it. It took me a long time to learn that lesson, but I'm keen to hang on to it now I've learned it.

## ⊕ THINGS YOU COULD TRY

Here are some things you could try if you'd like to apply this lesson to your own life:

1.  **Make a record of your own wishes** – Tom and I have made a lot of our wishes known in our will. The record that I had for my grandfather was incredibly helpful and is certainly something I'd like to replicate well ahead of time with my own children.

2.  **Talk about death and dying with older friends and relatives** – I've often found that older people are a lot less squeamish about death and dying than the rest of us and that while we might shy away from these conversations, they might welcome them. It may be a little awkward but, particularly if you're the next of kin, a few minutes of awkwardness will be well worth it for a lifetime of certainty that you did the right thing when the time came.

    *Make a start by* noting down anyone who you think you need to talk to about death and dying:

    . . . . . . . . . . . . . . . . . . . . . . . . . . . . . . . . . . . . . . . . . . . . . . . . . . . . . . . . . . . . .

. . . . . . . . . . . . . . . . . . . . . . . . . . . . . . . . . . . . . . . . . . . . . . . . . . . . . . .

. . . . . . . . . . . . . . . . . . . . . . . . . . . . . . . . . . . . . . . . . . . . . . . . . . . . . . .

3.  **Be braver in your conversations** – every now and then the opportunity to talk about death and dying will naturally come up. Rather than it having to be a 'Big Conversation' at some point, perhaps it is better to approach it little and often. Maybe a song you'd love to have played at your funeral comes on the radio or maybe the funeral of a loved one prompts you to consider your own one day. Whatever the stimulus, be prepared to run with it if it opens up these tricky conversations in good time.

# Say the things you need to say

When someone is dying, you have the perfect opportunity to say the things you need to say...but maybe you don't need to wait until they're dying.

### What I got wrong in the past

I have often been guilty of carrying a multitude of thoughts in my head which have never been voiced aloud. After years of hiding how I feel and blunting my emotions, having open and honest conversations with those I loved the most, even in their dying days, was not a thing that came easily. In fact, it hadn't even occurred to me that I could, let alone that I should.

### The lesson and the teacher

When Grandpa was in hospital, as his legal next of kin I was asked to sign the papers to allow him to be put on a palliative care pathway. I was essentially signing his life away and giving my permission for him to die.

It was exactly the right thing to do and I was following his wishes exactly, but it was one of the hardest things I've ever done. I'd been at his bedside for hours every day for weeks, but I took a break at that moment and went to my car and I wept and I wept and I wept. As I often do in moments of high distress, I picked up the phone to my good friend Joe and, between big heaving sobs, I unburdened all the thoughts in my head. I told him all the reasons I loved Grandpa and just how much I'd miss him when he was gone.

Joe, who can be beautifully direct when needed, told me to get off the phone and go and tell it to Grandpa, that I didn't have long left and that Grandpa, not Joe, needed to hear all these things.

I was worried that it was not okay to share such raw emotions with a man in his dying days. Joe reassured me that it was the right thing to do and so I composed myself just enough and I told Grandpa everything I'd not told him so far.

He was drifting in and out of consciousness as I recalled all the wonderful times we'd had together. I told him how safe I always felt with him. I told him all the things I'd thought and felt so long and so strongly about him but had never actually said to him. I said sorry for the things I needed to apologize for and I made promises about the things and people I knew he'd need me to look after in the future.

Nothing went unsaid, and once I was done crying and talking I finally felt at peace with his imminent death.

## What I do now

That conversation with my grandpa was a transformative one for me and has changed the way I think and feel fundamentally ever since. I've since had the privilege of sitting with my father-in-law during his dying weeks and, again, no words were left unsaid. He and I started the conversation sooner and it was two-way. We didn't know he would die, but he was gravely ill, and the words I exchanged with my gruff northern father-in-law who had the softest heart were precious indeed.

## Looking ahead

Following a recent conversation with Kathryn Mannix, a retired palliative care specialist on a mission to change the conversations we have around death and dying, I found myself wondering if I could be brave enough to have these conversations long before death. Why wait until someone's dying days to tell them a truth that needs to be heard, to make amends where needed or to thank someone for the impact they've had? In a podcast she recorded with me, she urged people to be brave and go and have those conversations. I thought it was a beautiful call to action and one I aim to be brave enough to take forwards in my own life.

## ⬇ THINGS YOU COULD TRY

Here are some things you could try if you'd like to apply this lesson to your own life:

1.  **Say the things that need to be said** – when someone is dying we have a beautiful opportunity to allow conversations to go deeper and wider than ever before. Empty your head and heart and allow yourself to be at peace with the person you love.

    *Make a start by* noting down what you need to say and to whom:

    . . . . . . . . . . . . . . . . . . . . . . . . . . . . . . . . . . . . . . . . . . . . . . . . . . . . . . . . . . . .

    . . . . . . . . . . . . . . . . . . . . . . . . . . . . . . . . . . . . . . . . . . . . . . . . . . . . . . . . . . . .

    . . . . . . . . . . . . . . . . . . . . . . . . . . . . . . . . . . . . . . . . . . . . . . . . . . . . . . . . . . . .

    . . . . . . . . . . . . . . . . . . . . . . . . . . . . . . . . . . . . . . . . . . . . . . . . . . . . . . . . . . . .

    . . . . . . . . . . . . . . . . . . . . . . . . . . . . . . . . . . . . . . . . . . . . . . . . . . . . . . . . . . . .

    . . . . . . . . . . . . . . . . . . . . . . . . . . . . . . . . . . . . . . . . . . . . . . . . . . . . . . . . . . . .

    . . . . . . . . . . . . . . . . . . . . . . . . . . . . . . . . . . . . . . . . . . . . . . . . . . . . . . . . . . . .

    The next step is to be brave and go and have these conversations.

2.  **Don't wait until it's too late** – while it's easier to talk to some-one who doesn't respond, if you can be brave enough to have

these conversations while someone is still conscious it's an even more beautiful bonding experience. Often there are things they've left unsaid too.

3. **Talk to the living not just the dying** – perhaps reading this lesson has brought to mind somebody to whom there are things you need to say. Life is sometimes short, so don't wait until it's nearing the end before you get a little braver and share those thoughts, questions or apologies.

   *Make a start by* noting down anyone in your life whose death would sadden you but who you've not been in touch with for a long time:

   1. . . . . . . . . . . . . . . . . . . . . . . . . . . . . . . . . . . . . . . . . . . . . . . . . . . . .

   2. . . . . . . . . . . . . . . . . . . . . . . . . . . . . . . . . . . . . . . . . . . . . . . . . . . . .

   3. . . . . . . . . . . . . . . . . . . . . . . . . . . . . . . . . . . . . . . . . . . . . . . . . . . . .

   Your next step is to reach out to them.

# Make memories up until the last moment

The last weeks, days or hours of a loved one's life are not a time when we stop making memories but a time when we can make some of the most precious memories of all.

## What I got wrong in the past

I used to find the closing chapters of loved one's lives very hard and thought that these times were ones I'd want to forget, but sometimes the very last pages of someone's story can prove to be some of the most precious of all.

## The lesson and the teacher

It was a geriatric consultant called Ailsa who taught me this most precious lesson. We return to my grandpa's deathbed where I find myself thinking that all the memories I'll want to treasure have now been made. But I was wrong, there were one or two very precious ones left to make, with Ailsa's help.

It was Ailsa who'd had me sign the palliative care paperwork. She was different from other staff because she always spoke to Grandpa as well as me, assuming that on some level he may be listening. I'd noticed even before his decline that being elderly somehow made people stop seeing him. 'How does he take his tea?' I was asked. 'I take it with milk and no sugar, thank you' came his curt reply. There were many such interactions and Ailsa was like a breath of fresh air, including him, talking with him, not just about him.

In his very final days, when consciousness was the exception rather than the norm, Grandpa woke one morning and asked if I would bring him Kentucky Fried Chicken. He'd grown a taste for it when my daughters introduced him to it. He'd not eaten in days and I wasn't sure how suitable it would be for him, but Ailsa sent me straight on my way, saying if he wanted it, he should have it.

He didn't eat a lot, but he savoured every little bite of popcorn chicken and had a big grin on his face. With just a little more energy after his unconventional meal, he perked up a bit that day and later on he said he'd kill for a glass of whisky. He was a big whisky fan and used to slip me £20 to buy him a bottle of scotch every week when he was in the nursing home. (Hilariously, it was the same £20. I used to put it back in his wallet when he wasn't looking and he'd give it to me again the next week. He never did ask why his wallet never emptied.)

He'd not had a drop of whisky in the weeks he'd been in hospital. I felt almost too embarrassed to ask, but keen to try to carry out Grandpa's wishes, I approached Ailsa saying I knew it probably wasn't good for him but that he'd said he'd really like a glass of whisky. 'At this stage,' said Ailsa, 'you give your grandaddy whatever he wants.' Again she sent me on my way. As I walked across the ward she called after me, 'Just so long as it's a decent single malt.' And so the very last thing Grandpa ever tasted was indeed a decent single malt, from one of his favourite little cut-glass nine-ounce rummer whisky glasses that I'd gifted him years before. He could not drink a lot and I had to help him hold the glass, but again, he smiled, right to his eyes while he lightly gripped my spare hand with his. It was a beautiful moment that felt just slightly elicit, which was so fitting as he was always just a little daring when it came to the rules. Shortly after that, he lapsed into unconsciousness for the last time and I've held that memory tight for years and years. I can still hear Ailsa's voice calling for a decent single malt after all this time.

## What I do now

I know now that so long as there is life, there are memories to be made. Those last moments can sometimes give rise to some of the most precious memories of all. When my father-in-law died, the very last time he was conscious, Tom, the girls and I were visiting him. The girls were dressed up for World War II day at school and they sat beside him telling him lots of stories about their day. He was so happy and I'm so glad that we allowed that memory to be made – it was Grandpa and the whisky that laid the groundwork for it. I'm sure that a different version of me would have decided it was not appropriate to take the girls, dressed up and excited to visit their very poorly grandad. That memory is one we all return to when thinking of him.

## Looking ahead

I'll try always in future to aid the memory-making process, right until the end. One thing I didn't do when the girls visited their grandad that day was to take a photo. Photos are such an important way of hanging on to memories but it somehow feels wrong to take them when people are very poorly. I dearly wish I had a photo of that day now, though, and in future I will try to better record and document these memories rather than just letting them happen. One quick snap would do; I wouldn't want to take away from the making of the memories, but a little something just to help cement that moment's place in history is something I'll try to do another time.

## ⊕ THINGS YOU COULD TRY

Here are some things you could try if you'd like to apply this lesson to your own life:

1.  **Remember that it's never too late to make a memory** – so long as someone is alive there is the potential to make new memories.

2. **Record precious moments in writing or with a photograph** – it's much easier to hold on to memories we have a record of.

   *Make a start by* noting down a precious memory you'd like to hang on to long after the person you made it with is gone:

   . . . . . . . . . . . . . . . . . . . . . . . . . . . . . . . . . . . . . . . . . . . . . . . . . . . . . . . .

   . . . . . . . . . . . . . . . . . . . . . . . . . . . . . . . . . . . . . . . . . . . . . . . . . . . . . . . .

   . . . . . . . . . . . . . . . . . . . . . . . . . . . . . . . . . . . . . . . . . . . . . . . . . . . . . . . .

   . . . . . . . . . . . . . . . . . . . . . . . . . . . . . . . . . . . . . . . . . . . . . . . . . . . . . . . .

3. **Think about lasts** – it always makes me smile to think that the last thing Grandpa tasted was a fine single malt. His last words to me were 'Thank you' and my last to him were 'I love you'. We hold on to these lasts for a lifetime after the death of a loved one, so a moment or two thinking about them will be time well spent.

# Dying is usually a peaceful process

Natural death follows a typical pattern and is usually a very peaceful process. Understanding a little about what is happening can be deeply reassuring.

## What I got wrong in the past

I used to be scared of death. In particular, when sitting with relatives who experienced 'death rattle' breathing or who might seem to moan or mumble, I used to assume that what I was seeing were signs of distress and that they must be in pain or uncomfortable.

## The lesson and the teacher

The wonderful Kathryn Mannix was the teacher of this lesson. As a palliative care specialist she's had the privilege of accompanying thousands of people in their dying weeks, days and minutes. She has now retired from that work but still works tirelessly with the aim of changing the conversations we have about death and dying and the way that we approach death as a society. Her book *With the End in Mind*[1] is one of the most impactful books I have ever read and that, along with the subsequent conversation we had for my podcast, has really helped me to understand death better and to feel more at peace with deaths I've been present for in the past, and will make me feel far more confident sitting with people as they die in the future.

---

1 Mannix, K. (2017) *With the End in Mind: Dying, Death, and Wisdom in an Age of Denial.* London: HarperCollins.

The book is rich and so deep, I'd highly recommend it. The key lesson I took from it is that death is a natural process with recognizable stages that we see again and again. Like birth, death follows different stages which can come close together for some people and further apart for others. But there is a progression towards end of life and understanding what is actually going on, and becoming more familiar with the process can help us to feel more at peace with it.

In particular, I found that understanding what causes the 'death rattle' and the signs that we might misinterpret as distress was helpful to me. Kathryn explains that as we grow closer to death we grow more and more relaxed and slip deeper into unconsciousness. As we grow very relaxed, we become so much so that we don't notice that irritating tickly feeling that would usually cause us to clear our throats if a little saliva or phlegm had collected there. Too relaxed to clear our throat, the saliva collects and breaths bubble through this, causing the death rattle that we so often hear as people come very close to death. Many people, myself included, assume this to be a sign of distress, of someone who needs help when, in fact, it's a sign of someone who is deeply, deeply relaxed and probably also very comfortable.

This is one of those things that I wish I'd known more about in the past as it's so distressing to see a loved one seeming to die uncomfortably. The more I learned from Kathryn about the process of natural death, the more at ease I felt with it.

## What I do now

I have never been one to shy away from deathbeds, but I'll be forever grateful to Kathryn for helping me to understand better the physical process of dying. It really is worth familiarizing yourself with this before you find yourself in this situation and I am confident I'll feel far more at peace with the process the next time I have the privilege of accompanying someone through their final chapter.

## Looking ahead

I feel passionately that we need to talk more about death and dying. I'm keen to share Kathryn's work and to do a little to educate people myself. With so many possible themes I could have included in this book, the choice to include a section on death and dying was a very purposeful one.

 **THINGS YOU COULD TRY**

Here are some things you could try if you'd like to apply this lesson to your own life:

1. **Familiarize yourself with the process of death** – Kathryn Mannix's book, *With the End in Mind*, explains it brilliantly. She also described it when she spoke on my podcast *Pooky Ponders*.

2. **Be curious about the process of death and don't assume the worst** – if you have the privilege of spending time with someone who is dying, be curious about what is happening. So long as any underlying symptoms are being managed it is usually a painless and peaceful process but one which is very open to misinterpretation. If you don't know what's going on, ask a doctor or nurse. They will have seen this many times before and will be able to offer explanations and reassurance. They often will not think to explain the process of death unless you ask them, so if you have questions, pipe up.

3. **Share what you learn with others** – as you learn a little more about dying and perhaps feel a little bit more comfortable about this perfectly natural process, think about who else needs to know and how you could open up this discussion with them.

   *Make a start by* noting down the people you think would benefit from knowing about this too:

   1. . . . . . . . . . . . . . . . . . . . . . . . . . . . . . . . . . . . . . . . . . . . . . . . . . . . . . . . . . . . . .

**2.** ........................................................

**3.** ........................................................

# Not allowing grief to happen doesn't make it go away

If we don't allow the process of grief to happen at the time of a bereavement, that grief will sit like a ticking time bomb and can explode when we least expect it.

## What I got wrong in the past

I had a loss in my teenage years that I never allowed myself to grieve. I boxed it up and blocked it out and pretended that it had not happened. For years, I spoke to no one about it though this shadow walked by my side each day. I was never unaware of my loss but also never allowed myself to fully process it or find any kind of closure. I simply pushed it away, took all sorts of measures to numb my feelings and tried to manage alone.

For years, this kind of worked, until almost two decades later, an event triggered my grief which was every bit as raw and real as if I'd only just experienced the loss. But having bottled it up for so very long, that grief came exploding into my life with the force of a hurricane and was one of the triggers for my spiral into several years of severe and debilitating mental illness.

## The lesson and the teacher

During the Covid-19 pandemic, I volunteered to record the priest of the church where I'm a chorister giving regular church services so that our community could continue to worship together online as they were prevented from meeting face-to-face. This meant that I spent many, many hours together with Grant, our priest, who has since become an incredibly close friend.

As a priest, there is little that Grant has not seen or heard before, and when it comes to death he's an expert in support-ing people through it. Although in recent years I've done a lot of work with my therapist about the feelings that surrounded my loss, I'd never really allowed myself to have closure, never marked the end, never quite been ready to move on, nor perhaps willing to give myself permission to do so. In his kindness and understanding and with the reciprocal trust we built after so many hours together, Grant was able to advise me and guide me and find a way forwards that allowed me to finally say goodbye, to forgive but never to forget and to finally give this trauma and loss from my childhood a shape, a name and a final resting place.

I will be forever grateful to Grant for the lessons he taught me about saying goodbye and about forgiveness and how moving on does not have to mean forgetting but simply enabling the past to lessen its stranglehold on the present.

## What I do now

While old habits die hard, I try now to allow myself to feel my feelings at the time that they need to be felt. I try to allow the natural process of grief to happen and I encourage others to do the same. I've always tried hard to enable my children to grieve well and I think that as a consequence they take a far more healthy and healing approach to grief than I've yet learned to. I remember one day when Lyra was about six and our friend Richard had recently died, she said in a very matter of fact way, 'This is very sad. I think we maybe need a cuddle and a cry.' And she was right, that was exactly what we needed. And it helped. It really did. Grief is a hard but very natural process and I often find that young children are far better at it when given a safe space to allow the process to happen than us adults who've often had our expectations of the process of grief bent way out of shape by society. So, if you can, keep it real and grieve like a child.

## Looking ahead

My commitment to myself here is never to bottle things up and never again to put myself in a situation where I am managing entirely alone, especially when I'm surrounded by people who are so kind and caring, if only I let them in.

## ⊕ THINGS YOU COULD TRY

Here are some things you could try if you'd like to apply this lesson to your own life:

1. **Forget the 'shoulds' when it comes to grief** – grief is a very natural process, there is no specific form or timeframe it should take. Trust in the process; we're very good at grieving until we learn not to be.

2. **Find the right way to say goodbye** – goodbyes are as much about the people left behind as they are for the person who has gone. These are the moments when we come together and collectively say goodbye as we laugh and cry and consider what life looks like without our loved one. If you need to find other ways to say goodbye or make peace, that's okay too. Find what works for you and go with it. Goodbyes matter.

3. **Do not put grief on hold** – sometimes we feel as if we can delay grief, just put it to one side until we're ready. For some people, this can somewhat work, and for many people it's only after a funeral has happened that the process of grief truly starts, but just beware that if you try to put grief on hold for too long, you may not be entirely in control of the moment it chooses to surface. It might take weeks, or years, but ignoring it won't make it go away.

# It is better to have loved and lost

The cost of loving is losing – the more we love someone, the harder it is to let them go, but that is a price worth paying.

## What I got wrong in the past

For many years of my life, I was cautious about forming strong and lasting relationships with people, so terrified was I of losing those people. It meant that I did not experience the pain of loss, but it also meant I did not experience the joy of love.

## The lesson and the teacher

This lesson goes with thanks to Richard, who I loved and lost. When my girls started nursery school, Richard was one of the first parents I got to know. His daughter Lula and my daughter Ellie were best buddies in all the world and so we too began to make friends. We'd only known each other a few weeks when Richard told me that he had six months to live. He said he thought I needed to know, as he could see we were likely to form a deep friendship – sometimes you just know – and he wanted me to be aware of what I was letting myself in for and to give me the chance to back out.

After a lifetime of working hard not to get too close to peo-ple, I had to do a lot of soul searching about this one. It felt heartless and cruel not to make friends because he was dying, but at the same time it felt unwise to walk into a friendship that I knew would end in heartbreak.

The thing is that Richard had such a magnetic personality

and we just 'got each other', so I couldn't resist leaning into our friendship and we spent many hours together. He had amazing treatment from the Royal Marsden and each time things looked bleak, a new treatment would come along and he'd fight to live through another cycle of chemotherapy. In total, I knew him for about three years before he died. When I was suicidal and he was dying of cancer, we shared an understanding of one another that was hard to match and we also shared the very darkest sense of humour. I used to feel guilty that I wanted to kill myself while he wanted to live but was dying. It felt wrong to talk to him about it, but he saw it quite plainly; his illness was in his body, mine was in my brain, we were both ill and we both had to help each other to keep on fighting.

He was just brilliant. And then he died. It was hard. But I'm so glad that I got to love him in life, even though I miss him so much.

## What I do now

Richard's been gone now longer than I knew him for and yet I think of him often, especially when I'm driving. He helped me return to driving after a long hiatus by having me run errands when he was no longer allowed to drive, and giving me driving instruction as we drove places. He always used to joke that he was the perfect driving instructor for me given that he was going to die anyway. There is a particularly tricky roundabout in Croydon and every single time I drive round it I hear his voice calmly guiding me and making the complicated roundabout seem so simple. He had a gift of making hard things feel easier. I miss that.

Richard taught me to lean into love even though the stakes are high, and any time I'm unsure, I feel the fear and do it anyway, knowing that Richard would tell me to shut up and get on with it.

## Looking ahead

We'll be relocating as a family soon. I'm hoping that the lessons I've learned in recent years about leaning into love and friendships will help me both to maintain the friends I've finally made in Croydon and also to be brave enough to make new, deep friendships.

## ⬇ THINGS YOU COULD TRY

Here are some things you could try if you'd like to apply this lesson to your own life:

1. **Lean into friendship** – be brave enough to feel deeply and to trust wholly, even though the stakes can feel high.

2. **If you have a friend who's dying, run towards them not away** – a lot of people are scared of death and dying and a friend in their final months may find that they have fewer people with whom they can be themselves. This friendship doesn't need to be about pity and sorrow, just about enjoying each other's company in the time you have left together. Sometimes the knowledge of death looming can lead to an intensity and honesty that you won't find in other friendships.

3. **Remember in little ways** – I talk about loving and losing in this chapter, but I don't think that we ever totally lose someone so long as we keep their memory alive in little ways. I often chat to my grandpa as I drive his little car around, Richard is with me on the Croydon roundabout, and as a family we all remember my father-in-law any time there is a change of plan as his catchphrase (to be said with the resigned sigh of Eeyore) was 'Things change'.

   *Make a start by* noting down the little things that bring to mind a loved one who has died:

   . . . . . . . . . . . . . . . . . . . . . . . . . . . . . . . . . . . . . . . . . . . . . . . . . . . . . . . . .

   . . . . . . . . . . . . . . . . . . . . . . . . . . . . . . . . . . . . . . . . . . . . . . . . . . . . . . . . .

   . . . . . . . . . . . . . . . . . . . . . . . . . . . . . . . . . . . . . . . . . . . . . . . . . . . . . . . . .

   . . . . . . . . . . . . . . . . . . . . . . . . . . . . . . . . . . . . . . . . . . . . . . . . . . . . . . . . .

# Dare to say their name

There is a tendency not to mention a dead loved one's name again for fear that it will evoke painful memories for the bereaved, but sometimes they want desperately to remember and it feels as if everyone else has forgotten.

## What I got wrong in the past

It is hard to know how best to respond when someone dies. What should we do, what do we say, how can we best help? For fear of doing and saying the wrong thing, often we say nothing at all. I am far from alone in having been guilty of this, but I did once get it very badly wrong and my silence alongside that of almost every other person in her life was heart breaking for a friend and colleague I let down.

## The lesson and the teacher

Our colleague Afra had a beautiful little boy who was born with a life-limiting condition. She was the most wonderful mother and nurse to him for the few short months that he lived. She devoted everything to keeping him safe and as well as he could be and protecting him from infection.

She enjoyed every precious moment with him and his life was longer than she or his doctors ever could have hoped, largely due to her devoted care and safe keeping of him. This was several years ago where the idea of self-isolating was an alien concept, but that's exactly what she did so that her Ludo might live a little longer.

Inevitably, Ludo died. The funeral that Afra held for him was one of the most deeply moving days of my life. None of us had had the chance to know Ludo in life because he'd been isolated at home and protected from all but the closest family for fear that he might fall ill from the coughs, colds and infections we all used to stroll about with all the time. Afra made sure that we got to know him a little on the day we said goodbye and put together the most beautiful video and picture tributes to him. There were a lot of tears and some laughs as well.

Sometime after Ludo's death, Afra returned to work and life. And no one mentioned Ludo. Not because we didn't care but I think perhaps because we were all too afraid we might upset Afra or we felt it wasn't our place to mention him, or maybe that we thought Afra would talk about him if she wanted to. I'm not quite sure why none of us mentioned him, but we unwittingly colluded in our silence.

One day, I checked in with Afra. I'd gone to work elsewhere in the meantime so I didn't see her every day, but we kept in touch occasionally. Her words struck me so deeply. She simply said with a voice loaded heavily with grief, 'No one will say my baby's name. It's like Ludo never existed.'

And I realized we'd got it badly wrong.

Afra wanted and needed to remember and celebrate the life of her baby as well as to mourn his death. What she didn't need was silence. Maybe his name would have provoked distress and tears, but maybe that's something we need to become more comfortable with.

Maybe someone different would not want to be reminded of their baby by hearing his name, but Afra did. We didn't know because we didn't ask.

## What I do now

Sadly, I have since had another colleague whose child died. I felt far more able to be a supportive colleague this time. I knew that it was important to have that very difficult conversation and ask a grieving mum how we could best support her. Did she want us to talk about her daughter or would she prefer we didn't? We had an open and honest conversation and we agreed to revisit it as time passed because what she needed and how we could best support her might change.

People need different things; we can't assume, we must ask and we must find out the terms on which they'd like to grieve, how best we can help them this week, and we may need to revisit that next week.

In particular, when a parent loses a child or suffers a miscarriage, we should be sensitive to how and how much they'd like to remember their baby. It's a very personal journey but we don't have the right to choose the direction that journey takes, and our discomfort and awkwardness about bringing up the name and memory of a child who has sadly died is not reason enough for a grieving parent or carer to have to navigate their grief alone.

I got this very wrong. Of all the lessons, this is one where I hope my failure will create an opportunity for you to do better than I did should you ever find yourself in this situation.

## Looking ahead

This is a conversation I've been reluctant to have because I've been so ashamed of how wrong I got it. But I realize that by not owning a mistake, it doesn't make it go away, as by not mentioning Ludo's name it did not make the grief of his death go away. I think that we need to have more open and honest conversations about how we can best support friends and colleagues who are grieving. In particular, I think we must learn more about how to support parents who've experienced the death of a child or baby either before or after birth.

I'm not quite sure what my role is here, but it's a conversation I'd like to help grow. This is somewhere where I think we can do far better, in particular when it comes to miscarriage, which is more common than we might imagine because so few people talk about it, choosing instead to carry their grief alone.

Grief is messy and hard but it's a far easier burden to carry when that burden is shared among many.

## THINGS YOU COULD TRY

Here are some things you could try if you'd like to apply this lesson to your own life:

1. **Ask simple, concrete questions of a grieving friend or colleague** – it's an awkward conversation but it will help you to support them better. Ask if they'd like you to talk about and remember with them the person they've lost and if so when and how. The onus should be on us to enable these conversations rather than waiting for a distressed and grieving person to come to us in their hour of need.

2. **Communicate clearly with others how they can best help** – if a friend or person you line manage has shared with you how they'd like to be supported and whether or not they want to talk about the person they're grieving, ask permission to share this information with other friends and colleagues.

3. **If you are the one who is grieving, tell people what you want** – the onus should not be on you as the grieving person to lay out how others can help you, but the stigma and awkwardness around death and dying often means that if you don't start the conversation, it won't be started at all. So, if you can find it within yourself, start the conversation. Be clear about what would most help you and whether you're happy for people to talk to you about the person who died. It can often be easier to write your wishes down and share them in an email or letter than to say them out loud. That also has the benefit of giving the person you're telling a written record of your wishes, which means they are less likely to misinterpret them or get them wrong.

# Part 6

# LESSONS IN LIVING WITH ANXIETY

# The first step is always the hardest

Getting started is the hardest thing of all. Focus your energy on getting started and often the rest will follow.

## What I got wrong in the past

Anxiety can make your world grow smaller and smaller and your head becomes full of the things you can't do. Feeling the fear and doing it anyway is rather easier said than done and I used to find myself shrinking away from all sorts of faces, spaces and activities that simply felt too hard because I imagined the end goal and how very far that felt from where I was now.

At one point, my world had shrunk so far that I no longer found myself able to cross the threshold of my house. I didn't leave my house for weeks on end. The world felt so big, so terrifying, so other, that I just couldn't do it.

## The lesson and the teacher

This period when I found myself confined to my home culminated in a stay at the Maytree, which is a respite home for people who are suicidal. It's a house in North London, full of love and care where people for whom life has become just too hard can rest, talk and find themselves held by the many hands of strangers who care. It's a wonderful healing place.

I went from my house to the Maytree, which was in and of itself a big deal, but once I arrived, I exchanged one set of four walls for another – until Joe came along. Joe lived not far away and had suggested we go for a walk one afternoon. The idea was unimaginably hard. I couldn't begin to think how I could do this, especially not on these busy London streets so full of people and cars and noises and smells.

So Joe suggested he called on me and I stood on the doorstep with him, and if that was okay we could take a few steps, and if that was okay we could go to the end of the street. He said I could turn back any time. It will sound bizarre to anyone who's not experienced this kind of anxiety, and indeed it sounds bizarre to me thinking of this former version of myself, but at that moment, taking that step out onto a busy street was the hardest thing I'd done in a very, very long time.

Supported by one of my very best friends and safe in the knowledge that I could turn back if I wanted to, I willingly stepped outside. I remember vividly the wall of noise that hit me and how the world felt so big and bright and scary. But here I was. Outside. After a few minutes, I felt able to start walking with Joe, and once we got to walking and talking, the whole thing became a little bit easier with every step.

## What I do now

That first step was by far the hardest and for me it was a very literal thing. Ever since that day, if I ever find myself retreating back to my indoor hiding place, I think about how I can make that first step again, safe in the knowledge that it will get easier with each further step. Having an incredibly supportive husband helps; often we take those first steps together each day. Even now in these days of relative wellness, I find that an early morning dog walk, taken while bleary eyed and before I've had a chance to think too much and am still simply working on autopilot, helps me to keep on top of my fear of the world.

By the time I have breakfast, I've done the hardest thing and the rest of the day feels more possible.

## Looking ahead

I try to make sure that I keep practising the things I find hard and am very aware that I can quite quickly revert to old patterns, whether that's hiding inside or not eating or not talking to people. There are many different cycles I fall into; I rely heavily on my husband, who is so incredibly kind and caring and is always by my side on a day when the first mouthful, the first step or the first hello feels almost impossible. I often try to stop thinking about the Big Thing and just wonder about what the first step needs to look like and how I can be supported to make it. I think this is a strategy that will continue to stand me in good stead and perhaps it will work for you or a loved one too.

 **THINGS YOU COULD TRY**

Here are some things you could try if you'd like to apply this lesson to your own life:

1. **Define your 'first step'** – this idea is not just about taking actual steps, but about getting started on anything that is a big trigger for anxiety. Letting go of the big picture and instead thinking of just the very first thing that needs to happen to set you in the right direction can help you make a start. It's a bit like someone with writer's block being faced with a beautiful blank new notebook. The blank page is intimidating, but as soon as we stop the page being blank, the process becomes more manageable. We don't have to un-blank it with perfect prose or poetry; copying out a quote, writing a sentence about our day or simply doodling is a start, makes the page feel less blank and intimidating and opens the gateway to the next step.

   *Make a start by* thinking about a current anxiety and noting the first, tiny, steps you could take to get started:

   . . . . . . . . . . . . . . . . . . . . . . . . . . . . . . . . . . . . . . . . . . . . . . . . . . .

   . . . . . . . . . . . . . . . . . . . . . . . . . . . . . . . . . . . . . . . . . . . . . . . . . . .

. . . . . . . . . . . . . . . . . . . . . . . . . . . . . . . . . . . . . . . . . . . . . . . . . . . . . . . . . . . . . . .

. . . . . . . . . . . . . . . . . . . . . . . . . . . . . . . . . . . . . . . . . . . . . . . . . . . . . . . . . . . . . . .

2. **Find an ally** – first steps are easier when you have a friend by your side. It doesn't have to be a human friend. My dog Buddy has often helped me be a little braver and take those first steps. I've also found that reaching out to friends online or having a friend on the other end of a phone can help me manage things I feel unable to do alone.

   *Make a start by* noting down the people (or pets) who make you feel better:

   1. . . . . . . . . . . . . . . . . . . . . . . . . . . . . . . . . . . . . . . . . . . . . . . . . . . . . . . .

   2. . . . . . . . . . . . . . . . . . . . . . . . . . . . . . . . . . . . . . . . . . . . . . . . . . . . . . . .

   3. . . . . . . . . . . . . . . . . . . . . . . . . . . . . . . . . . . . . . . . . . . . . . . . . . . . . . . .

3. **Do it again** – first steps feel far less hard the second time, and easier still the third and subsequent times. Practise the things you find hard and prove to yourself that you can do them. Sometimes it's helpful to remind those who are supporting you that this still feels really hard, because you may appear to be managing well. But it really will get easier with time and repetition.

# Cuddles are the best medicine

There are very few things that don't feel at least a little bit better once you've been held in the arms of someone you trust for a few seconds.

## What I got wrong in the past

Those who know me now would likely find it hard to imagine that I used not to be very tactile, but I was pretty slow to understand the healing power of touch. It's only as a mother that I've grown to really appreciate quite how powerful a hug can be.

## The lesson and the teacher

I had the most wonderful midwife, Melanie, who taught me about the power of touch. I was worried about not being a good enough mother, about not being able to be the mum my baby needed, and Melanie observed me rhythmically stroking Lyra's back as she slept beside me as this conversation unfolded. 'The thing is,' Melanie told me, 'you won't be perfect, no mum is, but you're the only person in the world who can stroke her back just like that. Look how calm she is.'

She went on to explain the science of touch to me and how human touch releases oxytocin, 'the love hormone', and there was something magical about knowing the science that underpinned those most natural of responses. As I've muddled my way through motherhood, I've found it amazing that no matter how distressed one of my children is, a cuddle does always help. It helps rage, it helps sadness, it helps anything that is just too big to manage right now.

## What I do now

When faced with distress from one of my children, I pull them tight and envelop them in my arms, breathing them in and waiting for their breath to match mine. This, more than anything else, helps in those moments of dysregulation when it feels as if things are about to completely derail. It has the added benefit of flooding not only their body with oxytocin but mine too, leaving both me and whichever daughter is struggling at the time more able to find a place of relative peace and calm and work out what to do next.

It took all of my resolve to use this method on the few occasions that one of my girls became loud and angry in public. It is hard to ignore the eyes of others judging your parenting as you envelop a child, who they might feel needs reprimanding, into a bear hug. But it worked, every time. Of course we talk about the behaviour, but not in that moment. Adding my anger to theirs is not a mistake I've entirely avoided but it's never ended well.

My girls are bigger now and beginning to enter those hormonal pre-teen years. Moods flip and friendships are the cause of ever-changing hurt and drama. There is little I can do except listen and offer a cuddle; most days that's enough. I too seek cuddles in moments of distress, having learned from my girls about their amazing power. In just the same way that I will ask 'Cuddle?' of my girls in a rage and open my arms as they snuggle in and allow the distress to subside, my husband will ask me 'Cuddle?' when he can see I need one. My distress is generally less obvious to most but he knows just when a cuddle intervention is needed. And it always, always helps.

## Looking ahead

As we begin to emerge from the pandemic, I don't know what the future holds in terms of touch and cuddles but I do hope we can look forward to a time when we can all physically comfort each other a little more. Perhaps now, more than ever, we've come to understand the incredible power of touch – it's certainly something I'm keen to explore more.

## THINGS YOU COULD TRY

Here are some things you could try if you'd like to apply this lesson to your own life:

1. **Cuddle to calm others** – in moments of high distress, see whether a cuddle can provide some comfort. Be curious about it; it really is surprisingly effective. As a parent or friend, holding someone close and allowing your breathing to start to match one another is a very powerful way of working through big feelings.

2. **Hug yourself** – if you find yourself craving contact but don't have someone to cuddle, cuddling yourself can evoke similar feelings. Closing your eyes and wrapping your arms around yourself and breathing deeply can trigger a similar physio-logical response to being held by someone else.

3. **Stroke a pet** – if you can't or don't want to cuddle a person, think about stroking a pet. This rhythmic motion and the delight of the pet can be incredibly calming. Many schools have told me about the magic powers their school dogs seem to have when it comes to calming anxious children.

# You do not have to fix things to make them feel different

When we're not able to change the fundamentals of a situation, sometimes it is better to focus on making Right Now feel just a little bit better.

### What I got wrong in the past

I have this urge to fix things. To make them better. To totally change the situation and make the pain go away. But some things can't be fixed, either because they're unfixable or because we're not the person who can fix them or this is not a quick fix but rather one that will take a long time.

I'm impatient and I hate to see other people hurting, so this inability to fix things used to frustrate and upset me and, if I'm honest, got in the way of me helping in the current moment.

### The lesson and the teacher

My friend Amber takes credit for this lesson. We met for one of our regular glasses of wine during a moment in life that was challenging both for her and for me. It's a conversation that we'll both remember always, and which ultimately led to some significant changes in Amber's life as she came to terms with the idea of leaving an abusive relationship that had trapped her and hurt her for a very long time. At that moment, I can remember voicing my frustration that there was nothing I could do to make things better.

Amber took my hand and gave me a firm but kind talking to in response to this – firm but kind is rather a speciality of

Amber's. She told me that the only person who could change things was her and that it would take time, but that right now she was safe and warm having a glass of wine with a good friend and the hurt felt a little more distant. She helped me understand that by accompanying her in her pain and helping to provide a moment of respite and safety, I was doing more to help than I realized.

## What I do now

I've stopped trying to look for quick fixes where they might not exist either for myself or for others but recognize the power of feeling less alone and seeking respite from difficult feelings or situations.

For the friend who is bereaved or working through the steps of a recovery programme, you cannot do the hard work for them, you cannot change the fundamental situation, but you can fall in step alongside them and allow them to feel less alone in their travels. And even the tallest, most inhospitable mountain feels just a little more possible to conquer when we have a friend to climb it with.

It's also possible to provide respite from a problem and to take a rest from it. Time away from working hard and trying to challenge and fix things can be truly restorative. That glass of wine Amber and I had did not change the situation, but it helped to fill her emotional piggy bank so that she was more able to take the next steps. Respite from our worries, anxieties or traumas can give us the wherewithal to carry on. That respite might take the shape of laughter or tears or calming or distraction or heavy physical exertion – whatever it is, taking a little time out from the problem can often make the problem feel a little bit more manageable when we return to it.

On a simpler level, this is often true of learning simple calming strategies to manage anxiety on a day-to-day basis. These hacks which might help us to take control of ragged breathing or calm a too-fast heart do not change the trigger for the panic and there is bigger work to do here, but if they change how we feel, right now, just enough for us to manage to carry on, then they are useful strategies nonetheless.

## Looking ahead

'Walking with' rather than fixing is a lesson I teach often now and I encourage people to understand that often underlying issues might take time to be understood and resolved or to begin to heal. In both myself and others I try to encourage running towards rather than away from the distress of others, recognizing that while we might feel impotent and helpless with regards to the situation at large, we're here with a heart full of love, a listening ear and maybe a hug right now, and that really can make a huge difference.

## ⊕ THINGS YOU COULD TRY

Here are some things you could try if you'd like to apply this lesson to your own life:

1.  **Forgive yourself for what you cannot fix** – this is the hardest step of all but accepting that there are some things that are simply beyond our control is a really important realization to come to. Once we let go of the bigger situation we can focus in on the detail and helping with the Right Now.

    *Make a start by* listing three things that are beyond your control:

    1. ................................................................

    2. ................................................................

    3. ................................................................

2.  **Focus on the Right Now** – instead of trying to fix the big things, wonder what you can do right now to make things

feel just a little bit better. Laughter, distraction, calming strategies or listening are often good bets.

*Make a start by* listing three little things that might make a difference:

1. . . . . . . . . . . . . . . . . . . . . . . . . . . . . . . . . . . . . . . . . . . . . . . . . . . . . . . . . .

2. . . . . . . . . . . . . . . . . . . . . . . . . . . . . . . . . . . . . . . . . . . . . . . . . . . . . . . . . .

3. . . . . . . . . . . . . . . . . . . . . . . . . . . . . . . . . . . . . . . . . . . . . . . . . . . . . . . . . .

3. **Walk with** – letting someone know that you'll be right by their side as they make this journey can really help. You can't climb the mountain for them, but you can ensure that they don't feel alone as they climb.

# Avoid avoidance or you'll feed the anxiety cycle

When something scares us, the most natural thing in the world is to avoid it. In doing so, we can unwittingly feed the cycle of anxiety and make it even harder for us to face our fear next time.

## What I got wrong in the past

It's totally normal to avoid what scares you and it's something that I did. A lot. The problem is that our natural instinct to avoid fear stimuli might be great at keeping us safe from bears or snakes or cliff edges, but when the fear is of people or the outside world then avoidance can lead to our worlds becoming smaller and smaller and smaller.

This is just how I found myself confined to my house, too scared to step outside for weeks, as mentioned previously.

## The lesson and the teacher

This lesson was learned in a workshop at an event I was also speaking at. The teacher was a psychologist called Ahmed and his lesson on the fear cycle helped me realize exactly where I'd been going wrong.

Ahmed explained that when we are afraid of something, our brain tells us not to go there, not to do that. On some level, it's like our brain is hypothesizing, 'Don't Go There or Terrible Things will happen.' It's often hard to give voice to what those Terrible Things might be and the feeling is quite visceral but the panic that floods through us at the mere thought that we might Go There can mean that we, naturally, avoid the situation.

But, when we choose not to Go There, our brain says, 'Phew...if you'd decided to Go There, Terrible Things would have happened. But you didn't and they didn't, so that was a lucky escape... Better make sure not to Go There again.'

And so we don't, and we begin to build a cycle of avoidance which is reinforced by our brain's belief that this is the only way to keep ourselves safe. Even though it's really hard, if the situation we're avoiding is unlikely to actually do us harm, the very best thing we can do is to find a way to Go There.

When we Go There and Terrible Things do NOT happen, then we begin to break the cycle of avoidance. We don't have to have a jolly time dripping with rainbows and unicorns, a neutral time is just fine. The main aim is to realize that we can Go There and, actually, the Terrible Things will not, in fact, happen. I have to bear this lesson in mind a lot when supporting my daughter Lyra, who has been struggling with school-based anxiety. The natural response when faced with a mute and tearful daughter is to take her away from the thing that scares her and that's certainly what the mama bear in me always wants to do. But I know that what is in her best interest is for me and the wonderful staff at her school to metaphorically (and sometimes literally) hold her hand and enable her to take those steps into school. Every time she has a good or even a neutral experience at school it quietens the demons in her head a little and builds her evidence bank, showing that she can do this and that it will be okay.

It's not easy, though, and this is a lesson I have to remind myself and Lyra of often.

## What I do now

That's all rather easier said than done and even knowing that I should go ahead and 'feel the fear and do it anyway' does not make that an easy thing to do at all. When you're paralysed by fear and your body is responding as if you're about to be attacked by a tiger, it is more than a little hard to find your inner brave and get on with things.

I've learned that the best way to manage this is by carefully scaffolding the situation and putting the right support in place. I use this approach whether it's my own anxieties I'm looking to tackle, or if I'm supporting someone else or advising others.

The key is to plan carefully enough so that you have the best possible chance of success. That means doing your homework, knowing what to expect, knowing all the who, what and hows of the situation and planning ahead for anything that could go wrong.

It also means stopping and noting your success and celebrating and recording that progress. Remember always that the first step is the hardest, so making sure that everything and everyone is lined up to increase the chance of success for that first step is crucial.

## Looking ahead

I try, increasingly, to notice when cycles of anxiety are at risk of forming for myself and for my family and friends. It can seem incredibly heartless to insist on facing challenging situations and I've had many crises of confidence over it, especially with my daughter's school-based anxiety. But I know what it is like to have a world that shrinks to almost nothing and I know that walking alongside her while she mutely and tearfully takes those hardest of first steps into her kind and supportive school in the morning is the right thing to do.

## THINGS YOU COULD TRY

Here are some things you could try if you'd like to apply this lesson to your own life:

1. **Find a buddy** – finding someone to help you face a challenging situation and cheer you from the side whether they're

physically present or simply holding you in mind can be really helpful.

*Make a start by* noting down people who could act as a buddy. If you're not sure who to pick, consider who you'd gladly do the same for in return:

1. ................................................................

2. ................................................................

3. ................................................................

2. **Do 'if...then...' planning** – actually planning for the worst can help. Write your worries down about engaging with the situation and plan what you'd do in each eventuality. Having a plan you can enact if needed can often bolster your confidence to go ahead.

   *Make a start by* giving it a go with a current worry:

   If ..............................................................

   Then ............................................................

   If ..............................................................

   Then ............................................................

   If ..............................................................

   Then ............................................................

3. **Write it down** – make a note of what you did so you can remind yourself another day that you took this step. Note down, too, who you were with and anything you did to make that step a little easier, and how you feel afterwards. Often, that initial anxiety passes and we find ourselves puzzled that we'd built this first step into an unimaginably hard mountain when it feels quite possible to do it again now.

*Make a start by* noting down what went well in as much detail as possible:

. . . . . . . . . . . . . . . . . . . . . . . . . . . . . . . . . . . . . . . . . . . . . . . . . . . . . . . . . . . . . . .

. . . . . . . . . . . . . . . . . . . . . . . . . . . . . . . . . . . . . . . . . . . . . . . . . . . . . . . . . . . . . . .

. . . . . . . . . . . . . . . . . . . . . . . . . . . . . . . . . . . . . . . . . . . . . . . . . . . . . . . . . . . . . . .

. . . . . . . . . . . . . . . . . . . . . . . . . . . . . . . . . . . . . . . . . . . . . . . . . . . . . . . . . . . . . . .

. . . . . . . . . . . . . . . . . . . . . . . . . . . . . . . . . . . . . . . . . . . . . . . . . . . . . . . . . . . . . . .

. . . . . . . . . . . . . . . . . . . . . . . . . . . . . . . . . . . . . . . . . . . . . . . . . . . . . . . . . . . . . . .

# 'No' is a complete sentence

When you say no to the wrong things, you create the possibility of saying yes to the right things.

### What I got wrong in the past

In the past, my mantra used to be 'First say yes and then work out how'. I think this was first inspired by Richard Branson who is quoted as saying, 'If someone offers you an amazing opportunity and you're not sure you can do it, say "Yes" then learn how to do it later.'

I'm not sure that Richard Branson is wrong here, and certainly stepping outside my comfort zone repeatedly has been important for both my personal and professional growth, but I'd totally warped and twisted the meaning and found myself saying yes to everything, not just the amazing, right, opportunities but all kinds of wrong ones too. I was always the first to volunteer, made myself incredibly helpful and worked tremendously hard.

This tendency to always say yes reached a crescendo when I stepped away from the security of full-time work and became a freelancer. Especially in the early days, I was so uncertain about when new opportunities might arise that I felt compelled always to say yes.

I was very productive, but often being productive towards other people's needs and agendas rather than my own. My approach made people like me and gave me some degree of financial stability as a freelancer. But it was ultimately unrewarding and contributed to repeated burnout and also to me feeling always on a treadmill, continuously busy but never knowing quite where I was going because it was never me who set the agenda.

## The lesson and the teacher

My PA Fiona has helped me a lot with this one. I am constantly overwhelmed with incoming requests for help and support. On the whole, I do my best to help where I can, but there are only so many hours in the day and sometimes I have to say no. This is easier sometimes than others, and at first, when working through the mountains of people who needed responses from me, I'd find myself either saying yes when I shouldn't or couldn't, or trying to soften my no with all sorts of reasons.

As daft as it sounds, it hadn't really occurred to me before that I could simply say no, and that that was enough. I don't have to justify it or give reasons why. Fiona has been training me and between us we've got far better at using no as a complete sentence. This is sometimes made easy, as people do make some pretty audacious calls on my time, and sometimes a simple no can be more than a little satisfying.

## What I do now

I am getting better at saying no and I've learned a few things. One is that by saying no up front, I am far less likely to let people down. I used to think that saying no meant I was letting people down, but in fact, I said yes too much and I went through periods of just about coping bookended with periods of burnout where I'd often be forced to retire to bed with a migraine that could last for days and would inevitably result in people being let down last minute.

Saying yes less and being confident in the yeses I do give means that it is rare that I let people down these days and I'm able to focus far more fully and give of my whole self to each thing I commit to.

I've also found that saying no to the wrong things has created space for me to say yes to the right things. Always saying yes leads to a very full and unforgiving diary and there were many occasions in the past when a really exciting opportunity would arise, but I'd find myself having to decline because my diary was blocked out for 12 months or more. Now I say yes less, but when something brilliant comes along where I feel I can have a lot of impact, or have a lot of fun, I'm able to say a resounding Hell Yeah!

## Looking ahead

The pandemic has helped with this as it enforced a complete clear-out of my diary. I'm committed to keeping it a little less full in future and to be confident in both my nos and my yeses.

Following the pandemic and our relocation and reset as a family, I am going to think very carefully about how I can be the one to set the agenda and seek out some things that I'd like to say yes to rather than always responding only to what comes my way.

As for saying no, I'm going to try to keep reminding myself and others that when we need it to be, that no can be a complete sentence. I'm going to strive to be a role model here and not to be afraid to say no, to try and let go of the anxiety, guilt, fear and shame that saying no can cause, because I know that I am far from alone on this particular journey.

 **THINGS YOU COULD TRY**

Here are some things you could try if you'd like to apply this lesson to your own life:

1.  **Just say no** – try it. Next time you have something that is a really obvious clear-cut no and you find yourself starting to write a justification for your response, have the bravery to delete the justification and just say no. Of course you can flower it up a bit and make sure you are being polite, but remember, you do not have to have a reason to say no to taking on someone else's agenda. It's kind of scary at first, but it only takes a couple of rounds of people saying thanks and moving on to realize that it really is okay to just say no.

    *Make a start by* noting down some things or people you would benefit from saying no to:

1. ...........................................................

2. ...........................................................

3. ...........................................................

2.  **Consider what you could be saying yes to if you said no more often** – reflect on what opportunities you've not been able to say yes to because you've been anxious about saying no to other things. These might be professional opportunities or they might be personal ones too. For me, the biggest cost of saying yes, especially to events that are unpaid or that fall in evenings or weekends, is the erosion of family time. When I say yes to the work, I'm saying no to my family. I'll never get to relive my children's childhood and this makes it easy to confidently say no to things that will mean I'll spend less time with my girls.

3.  **Notice how it feels when you get a no from someone else** – we often agonize over saying no and someone letting us down. But notice when other people tell you no. Notice how you feel and how long that feeling persists for. Most often, you'll notice an initial moment of disappointment before rapidly moving on and finding a different way around the problem. Saying yes to avoid this tiny moment of discomfort is a truly false economy and noticing how low impact a no from someone else can feel can help you to feel more confident in your next no.

    *Make a start by* writing about a recent time you were told no and how it made you feel and what happened next:

    ...........................................................

    ...........................................................

    ...........................................................

    ...........................................................

    ...........................................................

    ...........................................................

# Self-care isn't selfish

Taking good care of ourselves should be completely non-negotiable. Not only is it not selfish, it's also brilliant role-modelling for those we work with or care for.

## What I got wrong in the past

I gave and I gave and I gave and I gave, putting everyone else's needs before my own. And then I broke and my own needs were forced to take centre stage at the cost of everyone else's for a very long time.

## The lesson and the teacher

My psychiatrist, Niki, was tasked with overseeing my care as I worked through trauma therapy, came to terms with a diagnosis of autism and was trying to eat my way back to wellness following a severe relapse of my anorexia. It was a pretty tall order and I was fearful about how to begin to re-establish myself in the life and work I'd had to walk away from in order to focus fully on staying alive and getting well. Niki was quite clear that things would need to change and she helped me to think about the things I needed to put in place to get and stay well.

She encouraged me that before my diary filled out again with the places I needed to be and the things I needed to do for other people, I should fill it first with the things that I needed to do for me. In these early days of recovery, even mealtimes needed a long time scheduled for them as eating was so hard and needed to be supported. There were also regular therapy sessions to build in and the safe space needed after these to decompress and ready myself for returning to everyday life. She encouraged me to leave time for 'rest and recuperation' after such sessions and to think about what form this might take. It didn't necessarily mean rest in the traditional sense but rather rest from the hard work of therapy and allowing myself to think about something else entirely. That might mean a walk with a friend, going to the cinema with Ellie or going for a climb.

She checked on me often and I learned that in order to get well and stay that way, these things 'for me' must be scheduled first. It was also far easier to get everything else to fit around self-care when I put it first in my diary.

## What I do now

As time passed and I became more well, my commitment to self-care slipped as I believed that I was better now and I found myself filling my diary ever more and making less time for myself and more time for others. It didn't work. It just resulted in burn-out. There really is no shortcut when it comes to self-care and I've learned again and again that if I don't look after myself properly then I'm in no position to do my work helping others.

It's hard and I grapple with it constantly, because there is guilt and shame that comes with putting yourself first, but I must keep reminding myself that by proactively looking after me, I make it possible for me to be the best mum, wife, daughter-in-law, colleague and friend that I can be. It's not selfish, it's survival.

As I am autistic and live with significant mental health challenges, some people might feel that I need to prioritize my self-care more than others might, but I feel strongly that self-care matters for everyone. We all have a right to make space in our lives to do the things that keep us well and make us feel good. When we make time for those things for ourselves, we also give permission to others who look up to us – perhaps our children or people we line manage – to do the same.

## Looking ahead

The hardest thing I've found about owning my self-care is sticking to my guns. I know that my regular climbing sessions must stay in my diary if I'm to stay well. I know that I must make space to be alone and away from people every now and then if I'm not to burn out. I know I must make space to walk and talk with my husband, with whom I spend most hours of most days as we run a business together and have two children, but with whom precious quality time can feel a little too scarce at times. But knowing these things and doing them is not the same thing.

Defending my need for self-care and encouraging others to ringfence it too is very high on my agenda right now. As we all begin to question what life should look life after the pandemic enforced a massive reset, I hope I can encourage those I care for and work with to see self-care as something worth making time for.

We need to change the conversation and help each other to understand that sometimes the most generous gift you can give to others is to take good care of yourself, because only then will you have the physical and emotional reserves to be the person that others need you to be.

 **THINGS YOU COULD TRY**

Here are some things you could try if you'd like to apply this lesson to your own life:

1. **Consider what self-care means for you** – it's different for everyone. What are the things that help to restore you? For me climbing, singing, walking, knitting, time alone and quality time with my husband top the list, but your list probably looks very different from mine. Identifying the activities that help us is the first step...next we have to find time to actually do them.

   *Make a start by* noting down the things that restore you:

**1.** ........................................................

**2.** ........................................................

**3.** ........................................................

**4.** ........................................................

**5.** ........................................................

2. **Schedule self-care** – make a little time each day or week just for you in your diary. Block this time out as quality time for you to do the things that fill your bucket of sunshine.

3. **Use intention planning to help make it happen** – there is good evidence that clearly planning what, when, who, where and how we'll do something makes us far more likely to carry it out, so go beyond simply blocking out a slot for 'self-care' in your diary and make a very clear plan about where you'll be and who with, how you'll get there and what you'll do.

   *Make a start by* noting down when and how you can exercise some deliberate self-care in the next week:

   ........................................................

   ........................................................

   ........................................................

   ........................................................

   ........................................................

   ........................................................

   Your next job is to add it to your calendar and stick to it – good luck!

# Help people to help you

If you can be brave enough to let people help you and give them some guidance as to how, they'll often gladly do so and you'll both get a lot out of it.

## What I got wrong in the past

I used to think I should do everything all by myself, even though I was surrounded by people who were happy to help. I was always too busy pushing them away to let them help me, which, in retrospect, was good for neither me nor them.

## The lesson and the teacher

This is a lesson that has been iterative with many different teachers over time, as they eroded the wall I put up between myself and others with their persistence and kindness. Most recently, it has been my friend and fellow chorister Arthur who has helped me with this. He once told me that most people are fundamentally nice and will help you if only you tell them how. He's also been very proactive in trying to understand the situations I find hard and working out what he can do to make those situations a little easier.

His is the hand that reaches for mine if he picks up on the early signs of panic and he is the one who advocates for me when I feel unable to advocate for myself; this can be something as simple as ensuring that we all know exactly what to expect from a church service that is different from the norm. On the whole, the choir and the church are healing rather than harmful to my day-to-day wellbeing, but I don't manage change well and small changes to the order of things or what we're singing or where people are sitting can send me into a tailspin (thank you, autism). I spent a lot of time beating myself up for not managing better by myself but Arthur is always ready to point out that I don't have to manage on my own, that I'm surrounded by him and other people who care and that they'll all help me – but they can't if they don't know how.

## What I do now

This is true of other domains of my life too. I do all sorts of things that bring me great joy but that I find really hard. Telling people how they can help me has made it far easier for me to continue to engage with things I love. For example, if I'm giving a speech at a conference, making the organizers aware that I need an easy-to-find parking spot, a plated lunch and somewhere quiet to go and eat it, and a very clear agenda for the day will all help me a lot. All of these seemingly small things make a huge difference to me being able to engage fully with the day and do a really good job.

I used to feel like a real diva asking for this stuff, thinking it was only one step down from asking for a bowl of M&Ms without the brown ones (Van Halen's famous rider). But I've found that when I'm clear with people and I say 'I'm autistic, I find these things hard, please can you help me by doing X, Y and Z?', I am met not with reluctance or eye rolling but with kindness and compassion.

Often in life people ask 'how can I help?' and often we brush them off; but I've learned over time that people really do like to help. If instead of brushing them off, we ask something tangible and concrete of them, often that thing will be gladly done or given. I find this in my work too. When I'm grappling with a new idea or need more information on something, I've pretty much always found that if I reach out to someone who knows more than me about the topic and ask if they can help me understand a little bit better or share a little of their experience, they say yes. Furthermore, afterwards, they often thank me for the opportunity to share their experience. Talk about a win-win!

It's amazing. So many people are kind and caring and very willing to share their ideas and experience if only we give them permission and make it easy for them to do so.

### Looking ahead

I will keep asking for help in tangible ways. I'm not sure it will ever feel easy, but the continuous positive reinforcement of the kind response of others will certainly help, and in my personal and professional life, I'll be working hard to help people to help others to help them.

##  THINGS YOU COULD TRY

Here are some things you could try if you'd like to apply this lesson to your own life:

1.  **Accept offers of help** – if someone offers help, try to accept the offer and share a concrete practical way in which they can help you. This is especially important at difficult times; for example, if you're grieving everyone will offer to help and they actually really, really want to, but they don't know how. Keep a list of little jobs they could do that would really help you out. Maybe you need help walking the dog or picking up a prescription or doing the ironing or giving your children a moment to just have fun away from the grief?

2.  **If there are particular things that help you, write them down and share them** – this is something we often do for children, and it works brilliantly for adults too. For example, if you're someone who struggles with panic attacks and there are things that are really helpful, or harmful, to you in those moments, sharing those things with friends and colleagues

will help them to help you. You'll not be in a fit state to direct them in moments of crisis, so instead either have a pre-emptive conversation in times of calm, or carry a list of instructions in your pocket or on your phone that you can hand over in difficult moments. It sounds like a strange thing to do but it really does work.

*Make a start by* listing things that help you when you're struggling:

1. ................................................................

2. ................................................................

3. ................................................................

4. ................................................................

5. ................................................................

Consider carrying this list with you and sharing it with those who want to help you in times of need.

3. **Draw on the expertise of others** – if someone has expertise that you'd benefit from, ask them to teach you or help you or otherwise share their experience. People love to share their expertise and, so long as they have time, will usually gladly do so and be grateful of the opportunity.

*Make a start by* noting down three people whose expertise you'd love to learn from:

1. ................................................................

2. ................................................................

3. ................................................................

Your next job is to pluck up the courage to ask them. Remember, they'll be flattered.

# Part 7

# LESSONS IN LOVE AND FRIENDSHIP

# Treasure the friend who climbs in the hole with you

The friend who can meet you in your distress is a precious friend indeed.

## What I got wrong in the past

I think this is less a case of having got it wrong in the past and more a case of not having learned to get it right yet. But I have found that as I opened up a little about the ghosts that haunted me and allowed a few close friends to know the real me, I was surprised by people who had a somewhat shared history, of which I'd been oblivious. Often, they were prepared to meet me in my distress and talk a little about similar holes they'd been in and how they found their way out of them.

## The lesson and the teacher

Strictly speaking, this lesson comes from the TV series *The West Wing* and a scene that my friend Joe has quoted to me many times. These days, on a bad day, all he has to say is 'Need me to get in the hole?' and we both know what he means.

He's referring to a storyline between Leo and Josh. Leo tells Josh the story of a man who falls down a hole while walking down the road. It's a big hole and he can't get out, so he shouts for help. A doctor passes, so the man calls for help and the doctor throws a prescription down the hole and continues walking. A priest passes, so the man calls up from the hole for help. The priest writes a prayer and throws it down the hole and walks on.

Then a friend is passing and the man calls for help, so the friend jumps into the hole.

The man tells his friend he's stupid because now they're both stuck in the hole, but his friend tells him that he's been down this hole before and he knows the way out.

As you'll have gathered throughout the lessons I've shared, Joe has willingly climbed in the hole many times, and others have been kind enough to get in there too. None of their stories are mine to tell, but Amy, Zoë, Nicola and Arthur have all willingly got into the hole at times when I couldn't find my way out and kindly used their pasts to help me find my way in my present.

## What I do now

I've stopped judging people at face value and come to understand that there is often a whole lot more to people than meets the eye. Many people have a story to tell, and just because it's not tattooed across their forehead doesn't mean they're exempt from pain.

I've learned that the only way people know to help me out of the hole is if I'm brave enough to share a little of my story and challenges with them and if I give them permission to get in the hole with me. I used to think I had to find a way out on my own. But I don't and now I take my turn getting into other people's holes too, because although I don't know all the answers, sometimes I've got a few suggestions about different ways out.

## Looking ahead

I'd love to say I intend not to fall down any more holes, I'll certainly do my best to avoid them. But life is long and will, I'm sure, be beset with occasional challenges. As and when a hole appears, I hope I'll be brave and trusting enough to let a friend in, so we can find our way out together.

**THINGS YOU COULD TRY**

Here are some things you could try if you'd like to apply this lesson to your own life:

1. **Open up** – talking honestly about your challenges can put friends in a better position to help you; and help you they often gladly will.

   *Make a start by* considering if there are any people in your life to whom you could open up a little more:

   . . . . . . . . . . . . . . . . . . . . . . . . . . . . . . . . . . . . . . . . . . . . . . . . . . . . . . . . .

   . . . . . . . . . . . . . . . . . . . . . . . . . . . . . . . . . . . . . . . . . . . . . . . . . . . . . . . . .

   . . . . . . . . . . . . . . . . . . . . . . . . . . . . . . . . . . . . . . . . . . . . . . . . . . . . . . . . .

2. **Find your tribe** – if there is a particular challenge or issue you've faced or are facing, finding other people who've experienced something similar can be really helpful. Support groups (online or offline) and forums can be helpful, and it may well be that someone you already know and trust is hiding a similar truth to yours too, if only you can be brave enough to share it.

3. **Ask for help** – help is often the very hardest word of all to say, but unless you call up for help from the hole, it's possible that no one will know you're down there.

# Pruning out toxic relationships gives positive ones room to flourish

We can control who we choose to build and break bonds with. When we choose wisely, we can create a network of people around us which lifts us up, brings us joy and makes life a far more wonderful journey.

## What I got wrong in the past

I didn't always put my trust in the right people in the past, but one of the upsides of having a massive mental breakdown during adulthood was that it acted as a massive sorting exercise in the relationships I'd built up to that point. Some people stepped magnificently forwards and the bonds we forged during hospital visits and suicide watches are far deeper than ever they were before. Other people were notable by their absence. I was too ill to fully make sense of this at that time, managing only to be with each individual in turn as they kindly chose to spend time with me. But now I look back on it, it's a very interesting turning point in my life, and the resulting emphasis on some relationships and letting go of others has been a net positive.

## The lesson and the teacher

One of the people who really stepped up when I was down and who has done so many times before and since is Kevin. He is always quietly there in the background ready with a kind word, a guiding hand or a word of encouragement just when one is needed. Our friendship grew at a time when I was letting go of

others and I was quite distressed about the ending of those relationships. Kevin's kindness and uncomplicated friendship helped
me realize I was far better off being surrounded by people who
shared my vision and values, who liked me and who were happy
to help me limp through the dark days as well as skip through
the bright ones.

We don't talk every week or even every month but I know that
I can pick up the phone to Kevin any time, and he to me, and
we'll share an open and honest conversation that will almost
certainly be long, that will make me think and will make me
laugh too. A few days ago, I drove past a place we've often
shared a coffee and put the world to rights (a Premier Inn in
Central London, in case you're wondering), and as thoughts of
Kevin filled my head, I found myself turning to Lyra in the pas-
senger seat and telling her to make sure she chose her friends
wisely and was brave enough to let go of those who weren't
good for her.

She was a little puzzled by this sudden pearl of wisdom, but
as I explained the context she said, 'I'm glad you have a friend
like that. I hope I will one day.' And I hope so too.

## What I do now

I try now to lean harder into the friendships that really work for
me and to distance myself from toxic relationships, something
I'd been historically bad at. I find it very hard to socialize in
groups so instead nurture one-to-one friendships.

## Looking ahead

As I look again at my life–work balance, I hope to make more
time for the people who really matter to me. I'd like to spend
more uncomplicated time with people I love and trust. I hope
there will be more laughter in my future.

## THINGS YOU COULD TRY

Here are some things you could try if you'd like to apply this lesson to your own life:

1. **Recognize toxic relationships** – as ever, the first step is awareness. Are there relationships in your life which are unbalanced or unhealthy, which drag you down or wear you out or which are outright abusive?

   *Make a start by* noting down any toxic relationships in your life:

   1. ................................................................

   2. ................................................................

   3. ................................................................

2. **Let go** – allowing toxic relationships to fizzle out is often surprisingly effective. Sometimes they need to end with a bang rather than a fizzle, but either way letting go of what is not working can provide the emotional space needed for more positive relationships to flourish.

3. **Seek out the positive** – if there are people whose company you really enjoy or who you feel you may have clicked with, seek them out and create opportunities to spend more time together. This can feel a bit tricky and we're often mindful of the possibility of rejection; but remember, the worst thing that can happen is someone says no, and the best thing that can happen is the flourishing of a beautiful friendship.

   *Make a start by* noting down three people you'd like to spend more time with and get to know better:

   1. ................................................................

   2. ................................................................

   3. ................................................................

# Rupture matters, but repair matters more

We can often beat ourselves up for the bits we get wrong in relationships, but careful repair can strengthen rather than damage the underlying bond.

### What I got wrong in the past

I gave up on one of the best relationships I'd ever had because I thought it was irreversibly broken. I was wrong.

### The lesson and the teacher

It's a wonder to me that I've managed to write so many words without mentioning Jon's name until now. He was a childhood friend who I thought I'd lost forever. For years, there was a little space in my soul where he used to sit, vacated after he could finally take the pain I caused him no more and walked away.

I missed him horribly, but it took me years to feel brave enough to reach out to him, to explain just what had been going on in my life when I was utterly awful to him and to ask for his forgiveness, which he gave.

Jon is one of life's true gems, and if instead of quietly mourning his loss I'd thought about how I might fix things, he may have been absent from my life for less time. It wasn't easy to talk about my past – to explain or at least try to make sense of why I'd worked so hard to break our relationship down and why when he approached me with love and kindness I froze him out or ran in the opposite direction.

Not only did Jon welcome me back into his life, but he also

helped me to piece mine back together. While he'd not under-stood the whole story of what was going on in my life at the time things went wrong, he was holding on to enough of the pieces which I'd dropped or lost or blocked along the way to help me start to make sense of my story and to come to peace with my past so I could start to really live in the present.

## What I do now

I try now to repair ruptures quickly, knowing that things tend to morph and grow and become infected if we leave them, whereas open, honest discussions, heartfelt apologies and finding a way forwards together is a far more healthy and helpful route.

I try to put this into practice with my children as well as my friends. If we've had cross words, I try not to simply move on from them, but to apologize where apologies are needed and to seek to understand, in times of calm, what went wrong and what we could do differently next time.

None of us is perfect and we'll all experience bumps and blow-ups in our various relationships; most of these can be overcome, but only if we're brave enough to make an effort to repair the rupture.

There are exceptions. Abuse, of any kind, is never okay. Those ruptures are not worth repairing and some of the relationships I've alluded to pruning in a previous lesson were abusive rela-tionships. There is no guilt or shame in walking away from abuse. This should, I believe, be applauded and supported.

## Looking ahead

I will continue to aim to be humble and honest in my relation-ships and encourage others to do the same. Like so many of the lessons in this book, it's a work in progress but it's well worth the effort. And as for Jon? He'll be in my life for a long time to come. I'm hoping that one of these days we'll be able to make time to watch all three volumes of the *Back to the Future* films in a day, just as we did as teenagers but perhaps this time with our various children in tow.

## ⬇ THINGS YOU COULD TRY

Here are some things you could try if you'd like to apply this lesson to your own life:

1.  **Seek to make amends** – maybe this lesson has made you think of a friend who you fell out with. You may have thought it was too late to make amends. It's never too late, reach out, you might be surprised.

    *Make a start by* noting down someone you'd like to make amends with and why you think it would be positive to be back in touch:

    . . . . . . . . . . . . . . . . . . . . . . . . . . . . . . . . . . . . . . . . . . . . . . . . . . . . . . . .

    . . . . . . . . . . . . . . . . . . . . . . . . . . . . . . . . . . . . . . . . . . . . . . . . . . . . . . . .

2.  **Repair ruptures as they happen** – when things blow up, as they will sometimes, find time soon after to repair the relationship rather than allowing things to sour.

3.  **Revisit what went wrong at a time of calm** – we can learn a lot by looking back with curiosity at the moments when things went awry and wondering what we might do differently another time. For this to be effective, it needs to be free of high emotion and judgement and done with a genuine sense of curiosity.

# When you numb sadness, you numb joy too

When we take steps to block out feelings of hatred or sadness, we can end up blocking out feelings of love and joy too.

## What I got wrong in the past

I suffer with post-traumatic stress disorder, and in common with many people with a similar diagnosis, I've used all sorts of different strategies to try and numb out the pain of the past. I found it very hard to allow myself to feel the depth of sorrow, guilt and anger that my past carried with it, and my long history of anorexia and self-harm were in part caused in an attempt to block out those feelings.

Many people mistakenly think that anorexia is always driven by a desire for thinness, and, certainly, I have an urge I've talked about before to take up less space in the world, but restricting my food intake was initially triggered accidentally when I realized that not eating quietened the difficult thoughts that were constantly circling in my head. In particular, I had a compulsion to repeat everything I heard or read, backwards. It started as a small child after I heard words I wanted to unhear and my very young logic was that if I said them backwards they would go away. It went on for years and it was incredibly tiring. There were other tricky thoughts, feelings and memories swirling around always too, but I found that if I didn't eat then those thoughts quietened down. It was like magic for me. I no longer had to think or feel those things and so for years I did all sorts of different things, but mainly restricting my food intake, in an attempt not to feel.

## The lesson and the teacher

The problem is that you cannot selectively numb your feelings. No matter what method you choose, you don't get to say, 'I'll switch off the tricky ones, please. No more guilt, sorrow or anger for me, but I'll keep happiness and joy if you don't mind.' It's all or nothing. Whatever method the numbing takes – other common methods include drugs or alcohol – it's a complete numbing, a blanket over all of your feelings, rendering them all quiet and inaccessible to you.

At a very low weight I was in a state of numb retreat for years. I can't write about it too much because I find that I actually miss it now and talking too much about it can be triggering of those old behaviours, no matter how wrong that might sound or seem. But as I worked my way back towards health and for the first time in my life began to engage with a healthy diet and exercise, I found that my feelings began to change. Strangely, it was a cup of tea that Gareth, the centre manager at my climbing wall, made me that made me realize how things were changing for me.

At the time, I was doing very intensive trauma therapy and it had brought a lot of feelings to the surface that I'd not allowed myself to feel for years. This, coupled with the fact that I was now providing my body with the fuel it needed and properly looking after myself, meant I found myself feeling BIG things for the first time that I could really remember. The big things I was feeling were hard to manage – big feelings of sadness and anger that had lain dormant for half a lifetime and which I felt too emotionally immature to adequately deal with. I felt like a child, learning how to feel for the first time, and I found myself often overwhelmed.

The therapy was stirring up a lot of memories and I was having regular flashbacks and periods of dissociation. It was, to say the least, a tricky time. I was working really hard on not using self-harm as a coping mechanism and I had found that climbing was a fantastic alternative. It required such physical and mental focus that it gave me some relief from the many thoughts crowding my mind. I also found that the physical exertion and the frequent falls helped to keep me grounded and somewhat scratched the itch self-harm had previously been my go-to for.

As such, my trips to the climbing wall were frequent at this time, and I was not always in a great place when I arrived. One day, when I was in an especially desperate state, I walked into the centre, and Gareth, Craggy Island's centre manager, could see that it was a particularly hard day. He made me a cup of tea and sat me down. He sat with me until I'd caught my breath, the panic and the flashbacks were subsiding a little and I was ready to climb. He then picked out a project that he knew was just at the edge of my climbing ability and he gave me some hints to get me started and then told me to crack on and get climbing.

He's a very kind and perceptive person and this was not the first time he'd been kind towards me, but somehow, this day when I was suddenly more open to feeling all the Bad Things, I suddenly felt completely overcome with how incredibly kind he was. I felt a flood of Good Things and feelings about the simple kindness that Gareth was showing me. On a day when I felt that life wasn't worth living and I didn't deserve to grace the Earth, his uncomplicated kindness completely rocked my world.

After that watershed moment, I began to notice that I was feeling other Good Things more as well. As well as finally allowing myself to feel the hard stuff, I was finally feeling love and joy in a way that I couldn't remember ever feeling them before.

It had simply never occurred to me before that in striving so hard to be emotionally blunted, I had blunted *all* the emotions, not just the ones I wanted to. And so alongside my trauma therapy of learning how to cry, I was discovering how to laugh. It was a pretty intense time.

## What I do now

I still feel a bit like a child when it comes to feelings. It takes a while to unlearn a lifetime's worth of blocking tactics. But I try to let myself feel now. In particular, I try to notice when I'm joyful. I literally think to myself, 'Right now I am experiencing uncomplicated joy', and I try to take a mental snapshot of that moment so I can treasure it. I lean in to laughter and love but I also allow more complicated feelings to take up space when they need to too.

All feelings are valid; it's what we do with them that matters. I've taught this for years, but now I try to live it.

## Looking ahead

I'm working hard to own and name and share my feelings, to be an emotionally available adult to my family and friends and to avoid my natural instinct to blunt how I feel. I dare to love, I dare to laugh, and I've learned to cry.

## THINGS YOU COULD TRY

Here are some things you could try if you'd like to apply this lesson to your own life:

1. **Note if there are ways that you try to block feelings** – if so, what are the feelings you're trying to block and why? Consider what the pros and cons of this might be.

2. **Create an emotional safe space for yourself and others** – being able to simply be and feel is a really important thing. The safe space that Gareth created for me that day by making me tea and sitting quietly with me was not complicated, but it really mattered.

3. **Don't be scared of silence** – again, on that day with Gareth, although not a lot of words were said, a lot of words were unsaid. It's all part of the process. Whether it's ourselves or someone we are supporting who is working through big feelings, sometimes we need to step back and just allow the process to happen. We can have a big old jumble in our head that needs to be untangled, and a little bit of space and quiet to do so can be tremendously healing. Resist the urge to always fill the gaps.

# Sometimes love takes some time

Love is not always at first sight. Sometimes it takes a while to grow, and sometimes it's all the more precious for it.

## What I got wrong in the past

When Lyra was born, on the toilet floor, I loved her immediately. In fact, I loved her before I ever set eyes on her, but that moment that I first looked into her eyes, I can remember the instant connection I felt. There is a photograph of this first moment and it makes me ache with love each time I see it, despite the toilet duck in the background. Instantly, my fears about motherhood melted away and the meetings I had planned that day which I'd been worrying about during my early labour seemed inconsequential. Lyra was all that mattered.

In the coming months, we were jumping through the social care hoops to be able to bring Ellie home to join Lyra. Ellie had been born 15 weeks later, and although we were not her biological parents, we had fought incredibly hard for her. I had naively assumed that I would love her instantly, just as I had loved Lyra. But it took time.

## The lesson and the teacher

Lyra taught me about love at first sight, but Ellie taught me about a love that grows stronger over time. The very nature of the process of fostering and adoption means that you end up putting yourself on a pedestal for hordes of different people who are there to judge your potential competence as a parent. In painting this picture for the people judging you, you inevitably paint a picture for yourself as well. And, awash as I was with the love hormones new mums are blessed with, I was in love with one child and with the idea of a second.

It would be perfect, and they would be so happy, my almost twins. And it was, and they were. But not right away.

At the beginning with Ellie, we had a very unhappy baby, one who didn't know us, who couldn't be comforted by us and who had been removed from the only people and place she had ever known and handed to us. She cried a lot, she also vomited constantly and the medicines and strange milk she'd been prescribed meant that rather than that gorgeous baby smell we often find ourselves inhaling with a sigh when handed an infant, she smelt somewhat acrid.

It was hard work. This should have been expected of course, but it was a bump to Earth after the fairy tales we'd told ourselves and social services in the run up to her arrival. Her arrival was not like Lyra's. While we did everything we could for her and we'd already spent months fighting for her, I did not feel that instant connection. In hindsight, I wonder what possessed me to think I would. We were strangers to each other. We needed to get to know one another.

When I confided in my friend Colin, who had a lot of social care experience, that I didn't know how to soothe Ellie, who would become stiff as a board if you tried to hold her and would cry relentlessly with nothing seeming to make a difference, he told me that I simply needed to be there. He said, 'If she won't let you hold her, sit next to her cot, talk to her, reassure her and tell her that you love her. She needs you to care for her unconditionally and just to keep on being there.'

And so I did and, slowly, things began to change. She began to settle a little. We saw some smiles, she even started to allow herself to be touched or held or soothed. It was not fast, it was not plain sailing, but things were slowly starting to change. And then, one day, as I looked down into her cot and she smiled her gummy grin at me and she reached up her arms to be held,

I found myself mentally noting, 'Yup, I'd jump under a bus for you, Ellie.' That was a real turning point in our relationship.

I loved her enough to die for her. It had not been sudden, but it had grown.

## What I do now

My girls are 11 now and I love them with all my heart. My love for them has grown and changed over the years. I love them very differently but definitely equally. Lyra may have had a head start on Ellie, but they are both my girls now and there's nothing I wouldn't do for them. I look forward too to seeing how that love continues to grow and change over the coming years. Ellie has grown into the most cuddly, affectionate girl, so different from the baby we first knew. We just needed quiet persistence and a little space for love to grow.

## Looking ahead

One thing I did take from this whole experience is the need for more open and honest conversations about adoption and foster care. It's an incredible thing for both adult and child, but I feel quite strongly that we need to be more real in our expectations. A lot of placements break down and I can't help but wonder if the chasm between expectation and reality are partly to blame.

I am occasionally asked for advice from people wishing to adopt and I try to keep it real. While I don't want to put anyone off adoption or fostering, ever, I think it's only right for people to understand that there won't be a Hollywood movie-style ending. Love takes time to grow and you might feel all sorts of other feelings in the meantime. The feeling of rejection that I so keenly felt at the beginning with Ellie is one that has resonated with other adoptive parents. I'm so glad that our story is a happy one now and that we were able to persevere; as the Guinness adverts say, 'Good things come to those who wait.'

## ⊕ THINGS YOU COULD TRY

Here are some things you could try if you'd like to apply this lesson to your own life:

1. **Learn your love lessons from life, not Hollywood** – whether it's romantic or familial love you want to learn about, try to learn from real people and your own experiences rather than putting love on a pedestal and finding it can never live up to your expectations.

2. **Just be there** – if, like me, you find that it takes a little longer for a bond to form, be patient. Just be there, offering unconditional care. Make space for love to grow.

3. **Find someone who's been in the same boat** – if you're struggling, be honest and try to start a conversation with someone who might understand. One of the very helpful people to me during Ellie's early years was a friend called Joy, who is also an adoptive mother and had walked this path before me. Knowing that I was not alone in the complicated things I was feeling was comforting indeed, and the advice and support offered by someone who has experienced something similar is incredibly helpful.

# Do not over complicate love, simply let it be

Love does not have to be a certain way; if you simply let it be you might be surprised by the wonderful things that can happen.

### What I got wrong in the past

When it comes to romantic love, I made similar mistakes as I did with maternal love, believing, as Hollywood would have me believe, that it would happen all at once and suddenly and completely. It did not occur to me that love could grow.

### The lesson and the teacher

The teacher of this lesson is my dear husband Tom, who does not get enough airtime in these pages, though he was always by my side throughout every lesson learned. Tom's lesson comes last, but not least. Tom taught me how to love and to be loved and he also taught me that when it comes to love, from tiny acorns mighty oaks can grow.

At the point at which I met Tom, I believed I was unlovable. I certainly did not love myself and could see no reason why anyone else would ever love me. But I soon learned, from Tom's persistent kindness and care, that he did indeed love me, and there was nothing I could do about it. On reflection, I realize maybe he was to me rather as I was to Ellie all those years later. Now I think of it, there were so many parallels, including the fact he would sit with me quietly as I slept, so beset was I by night terrors at the time that I was fearful of sleeping without him there to wake me if they gripped me, and so, after my sleepless night, he would study while I dozed, waking me or soothing me if the terrors looked set to begin.

We were children really, when we met, him 19 and me 20, and the love that quietly grew then is very different from the love we share now. At first, I found myself railing against it. I still don't know how he managed to stick by me both in those early days and in the subsequent very challenging times. But he always has been right there, by my side, loving me and allowing me to love him.

We've grown up together and I love him more now than ever I did. The pandemic has brought us closer as we have had to work so hard to reinvent our family business, not only to stop it from sinking but also to enable it to be reborn for a different world. It's been tiring and stressful but a most incredible challenge, and has left me constantly in awe of Tom's intellect and his ability to learn new things and grasp entirely new concepts and make them happen in a way that quite simply takes my breath away.

Tom is easy to love, everybody loves Tom, but the one thing we are aware that we must always do is to make space for our love. It does not need to be complicated or jazzy, but we do need space to enjoy one another without the complications of work or family or the many things we have to do. We just need to spend uncomplicated time together, enjoying one another.

Somehow we never run out of things to say and somehow we've found that each challenge we've had to work hard to overcome has thrown us ultimately closer together, no matter how difficult it might have felt at the time.

## What I do now

I let Tom love me and I allow myself to love him. For years, this was all so alien to me that I simply couldn't let it be, but slowly I learned that Tom found me lovable even if I did not find myself so and that I could trust in him and love him and he would still be there tomorrow. That one took a while, but I'm so glad I got there.

## Looking ahead

I put less expectations on love now and simply try to create space for it to be. Whether it's romantic love, familial love or the love of a friend, I try to trust in the process and know that there is far to fall if it all goes wrong, but oh how we fly when it goes right.

## ⬇ THINGS YOU COULD TRY ▨▨▨▨▨▨▨

Here are some things you could try if you'd like to apply this lesson to your own life:

1. **Accept that you do not get to decide what others think of you** – maybe, like me, you think you are hard to love. If someone disagrees, perhaps it is not your job to persuade them to your point of view, but instead to let them love you.

2. **Make space for the relationships that matter** – love needs a little space to grow. Try to carve out time to nurture the most important relationships in your life.

3. **Love out loud** – if you love someone, tell them. We don't say 'I love you' enough. Tell your children, tell your friends, tell your partner. Show your appreciation for those you most care about; it will put a spring in their step and a smile on your face.